BAPTIZE

BY BLAZING

FIRE

BAPTIZE
BY BLAZING
FIRE

YONG-DOO KIM

CREATION
HOUSE
A STRANG COMPANY

BAPTIZE BY BLAZING FIRE by Yong-Doo Kim
Published by Creation House
A Strang Company
600 Rinehart Road
Lake Mary, Florida 32746
www.strangbookgroup.com

Unless otherwise marked, Scripture quotations are from the King James Version of the Bible.

Scripture quotations marked NIV are from the Holy Bible, New International Version. Copyright © 1973, 1978, 1984, International Bible Society. Used by permission.

Publisher's Note: The views expressed in this book are not necessarily the views held by the publisher.

Design Director: Bill Johnson
Cover designed by Amanda Potter

Library of Congress Control Number: 2009924878
International Standard Book Number: 978-1-59979-767-0

09 10 11 12 13 — 9 8 7 6 5 4 3
Printed in the United States of America

This book records the true spiritual experiences of the members of The Lord's Church in So Incheon, Korea, during the thirty-day consecutive prayer rally in January 2005.

CONTENTS

FOREWORD

How shall we escape, if we neglect so great salvation; which at
the first began to be spoken by the Lord, and was confirmed
unto us by them that heard him; God also bearing them
witness, both with signs and wonders, and with divers mira-
cles, and gifts of the Holy Ghost, according to his own will?
—Hebrews 2:3–4

Any Christian minister should dream of a grand revival worthy
of recognition. Likewise, I possessed a strong disposition toward
achieving massive revivals, and without considering the current situation of my own congregation, I conceitedly showed my face in a
revivalist meeting.

But as I started setting my service schedule, I heard the Lord say to
me, "My servant, Pastor Kim, your talent is not in leading the revival,
but in writing books. From now on, whatever experiences you and
your congregation members see, you must document precisely what
you see and hear. Through this I desire all the churches in Korea and
all over the world to wake up. This is the reason you were brought into
this world," said the Lord. I thought this was nonsense, so I opposed
and pleaded my case, "Lord. Writing a book just isn't what I'm good
at. Also, I have no confidence in my inadequate scholastic education
and knowledge." But the Lord repeated once again, "No. This is why
you were brought into this world."

I said to the Lord, "Why, Lord? There are so many people besides
me who can and are already doing it, but why me? Who am I, that I
must do this huge task? I am inexpressive. And furthermore, don't

You know I am not the type who can sit for a long time and write?" I tried resisting, but the Lord said, "No. You can do this. I will give you the ability. I will give you strength. Do not be afraid. I am with you." In the end I surrendered.

The Lord commanded me to clearly determine the purpose of writing the book. "At this present time the Korean churches and the congregation's interior and exterior faithful livelihood is in conflict with what I intended for them," He said. "The pastoral leaders and church members worship Me in formality and know Me merely in a written theory."

"What am I to do?" I replied.

"I desire that you have a burning heart and meet with me." This is what the Lord said, and it is distinctly written in Revelation 3:15:

> I know thy works, that thou art neither cold nor hot: I would thou wert cold or hot.

Secondly, the Lord commented on the true character and the tricks of the devil. He continued by recognizing that there are many books theorizing who and what the evil spiritual forces are. Jesus wanted to expose and document the reality of what unlocking the spiritual sight was all about, as well as documenting all the personal accounts of these believers experiencing real confrontations with the evil forces.

The developing spiritual experiences of The Lord's Church members' opening spiritual sight and engaging in spiritual battles are in all very rare occurrences. Though our church is a small and insignificant new church, God chose us because He desires to restore the unchanging faith of believers everywhere.

Thirdly, only through the word of our Lord Jesus can we experience victory over the devil's tricks and can we see the true picture of our faith.

> And unto the angel of the church in Sardis write; These things saith he that hath the seven Spirits of God, and the seven stars; I

know thy works, that thou hast a name that thou livest, and art
dead. Be watchful, and strengthen the things, which remain, that
are ready to die: for I have not found thy works perfect before
God. Remember therefore how thou hast received and heard,
and hold fast, and repent. If therefore thou shalt not watch, I will
come on thee as a thief, and thou shalt not know what hour I will
come upon thee.

—REVELATION 3:1–3

I suspect many readers will have questions, and for clarification I
have written down a few things.

THE PROCESS OF UNLOCKING THE SPIRITUAL SIGHT (PROCESS OF OPENING THE SPIRITUAL EYES)

I. Praying in tongues

Our congregation believes in the power of speaking in tongues, so
we were able to pray longer, more earnestly, and much deeper. Praying
in tongues also helped us concentrate, and with it came incredible
abilities that opened up our spiritual sight. Thus, speaking in tongues
is not for conversing with men, but it is our soul speaking the secrets
of our hearts directly to God (1 Corinthians 14:2).

II. Demon spirits will visit you

The process of unlocking the spiritual sight of an individual is not
only arduous, but one must overcome many obstacles. Amongst the
many barriers, the biggest problem is Satan, whose job it is to inter-
fere with and hinder that process. This devil has no sympathy for the
young in age or the physically ill. Instead, he will continually scratch
and tear us down until we are exhausted with disgust.

Therefore, if you are carelessly absentminded and inadequately
equipped, you will pay dearly. Many times we started our prayers with
a vague counter-plan, and when the vicious attacks came we suffered
a great loss. Now we, too, are thoroughly prepared to counterattack

by carefully preparing ourselves with praise, filling our hearts with the words of Jesus, and seeking earnestly by crying out to the Lord. Accordingly, the importance of winning the battle against the spiritual forces of evil was the necessary prerequisite for unlocking the spiritual sight (Ephesians 6:12).

Many congregations and pastors have the tendency to speak lightly about the importance of opening the gift of the spiritual sight, so I asked Jesus about those claiming to have opened spiritual eyes. The Lord explained that spiritual inspiration, as many people experience it, is an emotionally heightened state led by the Holy Spirit. But this is not the same as a person with the gift of spiritual sight who is physically able to see visually with their eyes.

III. The demonic spirits and their schemes

Compared to the fierce and severe battles fought for lands, the spiritual battles with the evil spiritual forces far surpass all our imagination. Satan's subordinates come singly. Then when one fails, two more approach; then they attack in groups of ten, thirty, fifty, one hundred, and even greater numbers. The groups repeatedly scatter and reunite to attack according to the situation. Then when one is chased away by a prayer, the evil spirit moves on to the next target with teasing, poking, tempting, and sometimes with whispers of sweet-talk. Finally, when their identity is exposed, they quickly run away.

IV. The demonic spirit's ever-transforming appearances

Satan's subordinates appeared before us in various appearances. Sometimes they would try to lure us by impersonating a famous entertainer, an innocent little child, a Jesus, or by masquerading as a beautiful angel of light (2 Corinthians 11:14). What is worse, during a church service one day, Satan staged himself as our heavenly Father sitting on His glorious throne, which almost deceived us. In addition, they came as snakes, a dragon's head, bats, a horse's head, dice, skulls and skeletons, and countless other images. They even threw us into confusion when appearing flawlessly disguised as my own daughter.

V. The Lord's method of confrontation

We fought and won, but also lost, many battles against the evil spirits. With our losses came agonizing pain in our flesh. The pain was so intense we rolled and tumbled on the ground many times. It felt like we were at the point of death. In the beginning, the Lord defended us from all the attacks; therefore, we prayed smoothly and without interruptions. As our faith grew, Jesus allowed us to fight alone and became a silent Spectator. Despite the imminent danger, we urgently requested His assistance. Jesus silently watched us as we tumbled. The reason for His silence was to train us to become independent instead of becoming as helpless children. After understanding the Lord's reasoning, we battled endlessly with the evil spirits. When we were faced with frightfully unmanageable demons, our Lord mobilized the Archangel Michael and the heavenly angels to assist us. Through this, the Lord taught us and helped us comprehend the proper fighting method. Ultimately, one by one, we achieved victory. Jesus wanted us to realize and learn that our natural disposition coupled with faith in Him could defeat our formidable enemy.

AFTER UNLOCKING OUR SPIRITUAL SIGHT

The physical fighting between the demons and us during the hand-to-hand battle resulted in bodily injuries. Even though we experienced both heaven and hell, the devil's forces attacked every chance they saw. Therefore, each day was a tense and serious battle in itself. I wondered why the devil and his forces continued to attack, despite our Lord's constant protection. I would now say that it depends on each believer's choice to either submit to sin or to Jesus.

> Know ye not, that to whom ye yield yourselves servants to obey, his servants ye are to whom ye obey; whether of sin unto death, or of obedience unto righteousness?
>
> —ROMANS 6:16

Our loving Lord assures us that we are not alone when we call on the heavenly angels to support us after we collapse from exhaustion following the battle.

Evil Spiritual Forces Attack

The evil spiritual forces are constantly seeking the opportunity to attack, but Jesus always reminded us to equip ourselves with daily prayer (Mark 9:29). It is necessary to have regular prayer. Jesus described the importance of praying in agreement with two or more witnesses (Matthew 18:19). In the instance when we received a special promise or an answer, the evil forces attacked us, and great suffering followed. The pain and suffering lasted a long period of time. The evil forces do not leave gently. Instead, they leave scars, and the suffering continues.

The Issue of Naming Satan's Evil Forces

Satan and his obedient subordinates have many names as mentioned in the Bible. Satan is denoted as "Beelzebub, the prince of demons" (Matthew 12:24); "Lucifer, morning star" (Isaiah 14:12); "Satan" (Zachariah 3:1; Revelation 12:9); "Devil" (Luke 4:2, 13); "ancient serpent" (Revelation 12:9); "great dragon" (Revelation 12:3, 7–9); "demon" (Matthew 7:22; 9:34); "spiritual forces of evil" (Ephesians 6:12); and "evil spirits" (Luke 7:21; 8:2). In the testimonies recounted in this book, we encountered endlessly expanding battles, and we simply described these evil spiritual forces as the devil, Satan, a demon, or the head demon. We ask that the readers be mindful of the fact that our nerves and energy were concentrated on fighting the battles; therefore, our names for each of the evil spirits we encountered may not be adequately expressed.

ISSUES WITH MANY SLANDERS USED DURING THE BATTLE WITH THE DEVIL'S SERVANTS

Test everything. Hold on to the good. Avoid every kind of evil.
—1 THESSALONIANS 5:21–22, NIV

While writing this book, one of the difficulties we encountered was quoting the foul language used during the bloody battles with evil spirits. During my daughter's spiritual journey with other praying members, the slugfest sometimes took place at the doorstep to hell. During the fights, many slanders wildly poured out from our mouths, but the Lord commanded me to document every detail, including the curses spoken. With a concerned heart I asked, "Lord, You are holy, but You command me to include the unthinkable curses in the book. How am I, the author, not to mention the readers, going to judge the character of this book?" Jesus replied, "It is during the battles that this happened, so do not worry yourself." In the end I obeyed the Lord's instructions.

I would like to acknowledge and sincerely thank all the Yae-Chan-Sa publishing staff, as well as Lee, Whan-Oh, for their support throughout our ups and downs along our journey.

I also must express my appreciation to my wife, despite our poverty-stricken life and many difficult circumstances. You encourage me with your unceasing smile and understanding. I cannot thank you enough. I ask the readers to read this book with a tolerant and generously understanding mind.

WITCHCRAFT SORCERESS BELIEVES IN JESUS

Sister Baek, Bong-Nyo's Testimony

A RED-AND-WHITE FLAG IS fluttering in the front door. When you see the flags in your neighborhoods, you may already know what they represent and what goes on in those homes. Merely two months prior to meeting Pastor Kim, that was what I did. Sorcery and witchcraft were my means of living and also my day-to-day life. I was not loved when I needed love, and my abnormal family life weighed me down. I was telling others their fortunes, but I faced an uncertain future with painful cancer invading my body.

I have one son, two daughters, and a granddaughter. My son, Haak-Seung (twenty-seven years old), has a Level 3 mental handicap. My eldest daughter, Yoo-Me (twenty-six years old), and youngest daughter, Yoo-Kyung, are Level 2 mentally handicapped. I was married with children, but I was influenced by the demons to frequently run away from home. My husband left and my children's lives became similar to mine. When I left home, no one was around to rear the children, so my mother took on the difficult task of raising them. When my mother died, the children grew up on their own, acquiring bad habits and behaviors. My daughters smoked, and my son became an alcoholic.

As more painful problems arose, the weight of my sins afflicted us daily. At the age of sixteen, Yoo-Me used my disappearance from home as an opportunity to move in with the forty-eight-year-old man from next door and had a child by him. After she separated from him, she met a thirty-something-year-old man and lived with and had a child with him. Meena, now five, is my granddaughter. A few years later, that relationship ended, and Yoo-Me found herself yet another man, this one forty-nine years old. Because of my choices, my children were neglected. It was my mother who took them in and raised them.

I had no idea what a horrible and scary sin I was committing before God with my fortune-telling. Before meeting the Lord, I thoroughly searched every great mountain and temple all over Korea in order to be possessed by the most powerful demon. I even climbed the splendid Hanla Mountain.

A witch or a fortuneteller usually uses instruments, such as a straw cutter, to tell a fortune or perform an exorcism service with prayer and offerings, in exchange for money. But I wanted more than that, so I climbed every steep, rocky mountain, put up my tent, and determined to be possessed by the demon kingpin. I start praying to the demon from the early hours of the evening until the next morning without batting a single eyelash. The demon kingpin, impressed with my dedication, supported my arms all night. Without sleeping a wink I was able to hold my arms up until the next morning.

I searched one mountain after another. I frantically searched, even though I had a family to tend to—but they did not matter to me anymore. I followed my desires. In doing so, it was the devil I followed without any hesitation. My family was destroyed. The children ran away from home and suffered psychological trauma. My husband left me. My existence was a living hell.

Finally, when I was diagnosed with uterine cancer and was hospitalized from injuries sustained in a car accident, God visited this sinner and extended His everlasting saving grace. Countless pastors came to evangelize to me, but not only did I turn them away, I poured out insulting curses on them: "If you can prove to me that the God you serve is more powerful than mine, then I will believe your God." I mocked every person who came to share the gospel. God, knowing my pride and stubbornness, sent a special pastor to me.

On October 5, 2004, as I was being treated for my injuries from my car accident, Pastor Kim, Yong-Doo and his wife, Kang, Hyun-Ja, from The Lord's Church, came into Room 708 of Sung-Min Hospital. Unlike many pastors who came by, Pastor Kim and his wife stood by my hospital bed just looking and smiling at me. At first I did not know that he was a pastor.

He looked so gracious and comforting. I wondered, "Why are they smiling?" Pastor's wife's first impression was good, too. He asked me, "Are you in much discomfort? You look like you're having a tough time. Where are you hurting?" He extended his hand and touched mine. I explained that I had hurt my back and was in great pain because of it. He shared that he, too, suffered from a bad back and urged me to recover soon. I was sure he was going say to believe in Jesus, but he never mentioned Him once.

In the evening, Pastor Kim and his wife came to visit me again. This time he spoke differently. "God loves you. Jesus is God's Son. When we believe in Jesus, He will lead us to heaven. Jesus desires to meet us. He gives us hope, heals our sicknesses, and comforts us. The sick especially will receive Jesus' love more abundantly," he told me, and invited me to accept Jesus.

> Yet to all who received him, to those who believed in his name, he gave the right to become children of God.
> —JOHN 1:12, NIV

He told me that we can go to heaven when we die, but we can also experience heaven now if we live obediently. I was shocked at what I heard. "How can you experience heaven while you're still alive?" I wondered. I was full of doubt, and I started trembling as my heart began pounding.

Pastor Kim continued. He shared that there was a time when he, too, worshiped an idol, but when he met Jesus he was transformed and decided to become a pastor. Oddly, his testimony was believable to me. "What is wrong with me?" I demanded of myself. I was so angry, arrogant, and full of pride. I shunned many pastors who came to share Christ with me because I was so confident that the idol that I worshiped was the best.

All at once, everything began to crumble. Finally, I decided to receive the Lord as my Savior and prayed with Pastor Kim. At that moment the tears poured out and suddenly my soul was at peace.

> Peace I leave with you; my peace I give you. I do not give to you as the world gives. Do not let your hearts be troubled and do not be afraid.
>
> —John 14:27, niv

Next to my bed was a former deaconess named Lee, Kyung-Eun, who stopped serving at church due to various life circumstances. At first she was in agreement with the pastor, then she said happily, "Bong-Nyo, if you go to church, I want to go with you."

The Lord's Church was a very small start-up church, and Pastor Kim and his wife were so happy to have gained two new members. But Pastor Kim had another request. He urged that any images of the idol must be erased at once. He demanded that I make the decision to dispose of my gold necklace and ring embedded with the Buddhist emblem immediately. There was a great sense of urgency. Many strange emotions surrounded me as I took off my ring and necklace. On one hand I felt uneasy, but strangely I had to surrender to this strong presence that flowed through and controlled me. Then Pastor Kim laid his hands upon me and prayed for me. I promised to attend church from that week, but Pastor Kim came to visit me again that same evening at 10:00 p.m.

As I was tossing and turning and unable to sleep, Pastor Kim and his wife came to visit and shared many funny stories. Mrs. Lee, Kyung-Eun was in the hospital bed next to mine and decided to join us in the prayer room on the sixth floor. Pastor Kim gave a service in which he shared his personal testimonies with us. He warned us that the devil might try to tempt us. He thoroughly explained how to prepare for those attacks. He assured us that even though we cannot physically see Him, Jesus is always with us and watching over us.

I have the kind of personality that will not quit until I have the answer. Pastor's wife shared that when she was diagnosed with stage-three tuberculosis, everyone said she would die. But, Jesus came while she was praying and healed her. I thought this was quite amazing and amusing at the same time, so I kept asking if this really were true. The desire to meet Jesus quickly arose within me.

Unfortunately, I could not keep my promise to attend church that Sunday. I could not make it because so many things came up at the same time. That Sunday night, Mrs. Lee, Kyung-Eun called me to share that her husband and two sons (one in high school and the other in junior high) all attended the service and formally registered as new members. They also attended the evening service and received a special gift. I wondered why she was so happy so I asked what kind of a gift it was. She replied that after the evening service the congregation proceeded to pray in unison. Pastor Kim shouted, "Your Christian life must be trained right from the very beginning. You have to experience it from the start." Then he held Mrs. Lee and her family and prayed for them. Immediately, their tongue relaxed, and they all received the gift of speaking in tongues.

I asked what speaking in tongues meant, and she explained that it was a direct, mutual communication between the secrets of their souls and God. I felt a hint of jealousy. When it came to serving a deity, I was a second-to-none servant. It did not seem right that I was not there. I knew I was missing out on something. I could not wait for the next Sunday to come.

I lived about three to four bus stops away from my children. Pastor advised me to leave the relationship I was in and reunite with my children. It would be good to start the Christian walk together with my children. I procrastinated in ending the relationship, but knowing that it was time, I left him and went to be with my children.

The house my children, Haak-Sung, Yoo-Me, and Yoo-Kyung, lived in only had some rice, which they received from the government once a month, and some *kimchee* (Korean spicy pickled cabbage) I seldom made for them. It was difficult for each of them to hold a normal job because of their mental problems. My son is temperamentally lazy, but with no family rules to implement correct behaviors, his initial reaction is to attack. I was nervous as I made the decision to go to church faithfully and live a better life.

Finally, the Sunday came when my family and I sat in the front row of the morning service and then waited for the evening service. Mrs. Lee, Kyung-Eun did not attend the evening service, so it was just our family. Pastor Kim spoke to me in the midst of his sermon, "You have to experience God quicker because you served other deities. Pretty soon the devil will tempt you, so you and your family must be equipped properly. Since you do not know anything about the church, just follow my lead and do as I say. Then you will have a good result. Are you going to submit?"

I answered firmly, "Yes."

"Sister Baek, Bong-Nyo, you decided to follow Jesus and brought your children with you. God will give you a very special gift tonight, because He is very pleased with you. Do not be alarmed if your body experiences something different."

I wondered, "What is going to happen?"

After the evening service, as the congregation prepared for the unity praying time, Pastor Kim asked our family to come near the front podium. He gave each of us a cushion to kneel on and asked us to raise our arms as we prayed. We did not know exactly what to do, so Pastor Kim led a prayer and we repeated after him. My five-year-old granddaughter followed pastor's lead quite well. "God, I am a sinner. I am a pathetic sinner. Therefore, I decided to follow Jesus. Lord, help us. Give me the strength. Help me experience You from this moment on. No matter what temptations may come, help me to conquer them. In order for me to do that, I need the Holy Spirit to anoint me with secret abilities from You." We repeatedly prayed these words out loud. The moment pastor put his hands on our heads, our bodies felt like blazing fire and our tongues rolled, speaking a strange language.

"Oh, what is this?" I thought. "What a strange thing this is." Suddenly, I opened my eyes to verify what was happening, but as soon as I started to pray again, the strange language continued. I realized my children, who were praying beside me, as well as my little granddaughter, were also praying in tongues. My body was hot, and a curious language flowed endlessly from my mouth.

My life was not always easy, but through this time of prayer I was able to ask for forgiveness. I cried out to the Lord over and over again. I could not believe that I could pray like this, considering it was my first time in a church. In the blink of an eye, two hours flew past. Toward the end of the prayer time, as Pastor Kim turned on the light, he asked all of us to return to church at two o'clock the next day for a special class. Retuning home we were overflowing with joy and we were busy sharing our blessings with one another.

The next day pastor and his wife came to my house in the morning to search every nook and corner for charms and disposed of them. In the afternoon we went to church and concentrated on the special class. We learned about the Holy Trinity: God the Father; His Son, Jesus; and the Holy Spirit. We especially focused on Jesus. We learned that Jesus came to Earth for us and to die for our sins. We were taught how to use the name of Jesus in various ways. Then after three weeks of education, my family and I were baptized one Sunday morning. (We were told that our family was baptized exceptionally fast.)

This also was God's enormous blessing for us. However, during the three weeks of learning about the baptism, my son, Haak-Sung, and daughter, Yoo-Kyung, took turns giving the pastor a hard time. Their ever-present fickleness was hurting the pastor's heart. Nevertheless, the pastor and his wife never gave up, but without ceasing they abundantly poured out their love on us. If he thought we were running out of kimchee at home, he would go to the neighborhood restaurants and ask for help. He brought kimchee and other side dishes to feed my family.

Without any discretion, my family and I sat in the warmth of our home and ate up all the food the pastor and his wife brought us. Other times when the pastor came to visit, my children refused to open the door for him, because they did not want to go to church.

My youngest daughter, Yoo-Kyung, no longer smoked and drank because she became a new person in Christ. My eldest daughter,

Yoo-Me, is in transition, and my hope for my son, Haak-Sung, is to stop his fickleness. Fortunately, he is making progress. As I look back, I understand how Satan tried to ruin and play around with my family.

My five-year-old granddaughter has many of my characteristics, as well as those of her mother, Yoo-Me. All too often she will hastily talk back and behave disobediently. Sometimes it is hard to believe she is only five. Despite all the problems, God never gave up on us. He sent a peculiarly special pastor to guide us to The Lord's Church.

I thank You, Lord, for Your love. I especially extend my deepest gratitude to my pastor and his wife, and I live an obedient life daily. I give all the glory and honor to our God. Hallelujah.

INTRODUCTION

Thirty-day Determination Prayer Rally:
Members' Transformation

By Pastor Kim, Yong-Doo

FINALLY THE DEVIL'S attacks started. The evil spiritual forces pursuing Sister Baek, Bong-Nyo's family persistently attacked, and she fell first. Her continuing back pain started worsening after her discharge from the hospital to the point of causing her to miss church. On the day of the baptismal ceremony, she laid at home with pain. I held her up by her arms and encouraged her that even if she felt like dying, she had to be baptized first.

Every day her children avoided me and resisted coming to church. The most difficult one was Haak-Sung because of his fickleness. On rare occasions when he promised to come to church, he would refuse to open the front door, pretending to be asleep or sick. Yoo-Kyung and Yoo-Me followed his example and ignored me or treated me inhospitably countless times. I thought of Jesus and endured each of their mistreatments. However, when the children were nearly out of food, without failure they opened the front gate and promised to go to church again. I was dumbfounded and could not believe what I was hearing. I brought all our food from home to Sister Baek's house, and many times we only had kimchee left for ourselves. I was like a beggar begging for food from all the restaurants I knew for Sister Baek and her family.

When I found a job for one of them, their speech impediment and limited expressive language got them fired. They were barely avoiding starvation, getting by with a one-hundred-dollar-a-month budget for their five-member household. The tiny basement room they shared was so far behind in rent they did not know when they might be evicted.

All too often the children turned again to drinking and smoking. Moreover, there were so many dogs in their already tiny home. Four or five dogs tore up the house. Their fur and stench were soaked into the children's clothes and blankets.

"Oh, Lord. What do you want me to do?" I cried out. "I refuse to be involved. I will not return here anymore." Throughout the day I was in an agonizing battles between my spiritual conscience and my human emotions. But every time I prayed on my knees, the Lord commanded me to go back: "Beloved Pastor Kim, if you don't go, who will do this work? What do we do for those poor and wretched souls? I don't want you to build up your sanctuary. It is good to have many members, but that's not everything. Go. Go and translate My love into action." With the Lord's words I cried out in repentance, and even though I did not want to, I went back to them.

I cried so much for this hopeless family. Frequently, Haak-Sung and Yoo-Me would manage to disappear to the PC game room or some other unknown location minutes before a church service. Sister Baek, Bong-Nyo's household was the scene of the devil's den. It certainly did not resemble anything close to a loving family.

In the midst of it all, 2005 arrived. Our church, as well as Sister Baek, Bong-Nyo's household, needed an escape. We decided to pray. I ordered and hung a decent banner to create an atmosphere. Our 2005 motto was "Be revived through prayer," and we began our prayer rally on January 2. It ran for thirty days. There were ten members total, four from my family, Sister Baek, Bong-Nyo's four members, Noe Sook-Ja, and another young man. I thought the sermon might be tedious, so I decided to make it as enjoyable as possible.

On the first day, after Sunday evening service, we had a prayer service. On the second day (Jan. 3) we experienced the fiery presence of the Holy Spirit. The unity prayers as well as the individual prayers exploded uncontrollably and continued until 7:30 the next morning. There was a good reason why it lasted so long.

The Lord allowed Yoo-Kyung and Sister Baek, Bong-Nyo to experience an awakening of their spiritual sight. After prayer service ended, we gathered in a circle to hear their testimony and exactly what it was like to meet Jesus. The other members longed to experience such a divine gift and could not wait until the next night's prayer service. Each member devoted their hearts in prayer, and I, too, desired this with them.

The duration of our prayer services became longer and longer. The Wednesday evening service started at 7:30, but barely finished by 8:00 the next morning. The Thursday night service started at 9:00, but did not end until 10:00 Friday morning.

God completely reversed our thinking. The more we prayed, the more the Lord impacted us with amazing things. Our Lord has prepared to surprise us with His many mysteries and grace and was waiting for us. "This is what the LORD says, he who made the earth, the LORD who formed it and established it—the LORD is his name: 'Call to me and I will answer you and tell you great and unsearchable things you do not know'" (Jer. 33:2–3, NIV).

All through the night we sang praises with a burning heart, heard anointed messages, and with all our strength we cried out to the Lord in prayer. Even though our service lasted through the night, no one complained. Instead, they longed for more spiritual food. The thirteenth day, a Friday night, the Holy Spirit came upon us so mightily that the service lasted until 11:30 the next morning. On Saturday night, since the next day was the Lord's day, we planned to end the service early. But contrary to our planning, the service continued until 8:30 the next morning. We did not have enough time to go back home, so the prayer team rested at our house nearby for an hour. We went back to church and attended Sunday service and then went back to our homes.

Day by day the prayer service progressed in this way. We were trying hard to finish no later than seven the next morning. These souls, who knew nothing of Jesus, attempted to pray to overcome their physical handicap and hunger. (They barely survived on one meal a day.) Our heavenly Father poured out His great compassion for them.

Both my family and Sister Baek's household were in a great deal of debt, so there was no telling when we might have to vacate our homes. Despite our bad situations, we prayed and persistently begged. The Lord visited us to wash away our tears. I do not know how I was able to lead this group to pray through the night without sleeping. They were amazed at themselves, and I myself, a pastor, was in awe of it all.

The Lord came to visit us while we prayed. We saw Him through our spiritual eyes, but at times we saw Him clearly with our physical eyes. Once on a TV broadcast, I watched two programs called *25ᵗʰ Hour Incident* and *An Actual Condition*—what is happening in our church was the real incident and actual condition.

When the service began, we all fell into excitement and deep emotional inspiration. As the children experienced Jesus, they were freed from disobedience and transformed into submissive, faithful servants. The areas in which they lacked were slowly changed into wisdom. My son, Joseph, and my daughter, Joo-Eun, stopped attending their afterschool programs and concentrated on praying. They repented of all the times they hurt us with their disobedience. Whether they were at home or at church, they respectfully called me "Pastor" instead of "Dad." Also, no matter what I said, they responded with an enthusiastic "Amen."

Haak-Sung and Yoo-Kyung, after seeing heaven and hell, cried on their knees and asked for forgiveness for the times they mistreated me. They vowed never to miss Sunday service no matter what happened, and formed a sworn sibling relationship between them. In sub-zero weather they went out to share the gospel while they blew warm breath into the palms of their hands. They headed out at four o'clock in the afternoon and did not return until after 8:30 with their hands and feet frozen cold. They insisted they needed to do more. They knew they had to be diligent because they saw their treasure being stored up in heaven.

At first my children did not talk to Haak-Sung and Yoo-Kyung, but recently they have become closer than ever. They see my home as theirs and come and go as such. Meena, the five-year-old girl, prays in tongues with her arms held high for two to three hours, and it is so commendable to see her.

Amongst the congregation, Sister Baek, Bong-Nyo; Lee, Haak-Sung; Lee, Yoo-Kyung; and Kim, Joo-Eun received divine gifts of prophesy, spiritual distinction, speaking in tongues, knowledge, wisdom, and divine faith. Kang, Hyun-Ja, my wife, and Joseph also received gifts of prophesy in the middle of February.

There are no falsified contents in this book, only the personal experiences of members involved with the prayer rally. Their accounts of meeting Jesus were carefully documented. It was a difficult work to put into words all the details of their experiences. Also, the real identity of Satan and his operations was about to be revealed to the public through this book, which brought about immense persecution and various trials. Due to the Lord's exhaustive intervention we triumphed, and He enabled us to avoid trials we could not handle in our own strength. I was tempted many times to stop writing, but it was in those times that I experienced the Lord's special comfort despite my deficiencies.

THE PRAYER WARRIORS OF THE LORD'S CHURCH

Pastor Kim, Yong-Doo: forty-five years old; is beginning to lose his hair more and more and shows symptoms of baldness

Kang, Hyun-Ja: forty-three years old; Pastor Kim's wife; former government employee with affiliations in congress; favorable temperament stood out

Kim, Joseph: sixteen years old; in the eighth grade in middle school; aspires to become a pastor; stubborn like an ox and reckless

Kim, Joo-Eun: fourteen years old; in the sixth grade in middle school; very cute and clever; likewise, has strong stubbornness and does not give up easily.

Sister Baek, Bong-Nyo: fifty years old; possesses strong tenacity; Lord confirms her "no one can stop her" personality

Lee, Haak-Sung: twenty-seven years old; Sister Baek, Bong-Nyo's son; Level 3 psychologically challenged; has limitations on adequately expressing thoughts into words, but mentally he is normal for his age; he is physically weak

Lee, Yoo-Kyung: twenty-four years old; Sister Baek, Bong-Nyo's second daughter; Level 2 psychologically challenged; to some extent she is slow in articulating speech, but her conversation is fine

Meena: five years old; Sister Baek, Bong-Nyo's granddaughter; her birth registration is incomplete due to inadequately prepared documents

Oh, Jong-Suk: thirty-three years old; he signed guarantor documents for his friend's loan papers, which turned out bad, and he was kicked out of his home; he was homeless and slept on the edge of the park's pond, where he met Pastor Kim, who brought him to church and found him a job; he stopped coming to church after he got a job

Deaconess Shin, Sung-Kyung: thirty-three years old; she only attended Sunday morning services, but started changing when she joined the prayer rally on the fifteenth day; her nine-year-old daughter has pediatric cancer

Oh, Jung-Min: eight years old; Deaconess Shin, Sung-Kyung's son; his hobbies included watching TV and playing computer games, but after attending the prayer rally he vowed to become a pastor; from the first day he received the gift of tongues

DAY ONE
God Helps Us from His Most Holy Place

The LORD hear thee in the day of trouble; the name of the
God of Jacob defend thee; Send thee help from the sanctuary, and strengthen thee out of Zion; Remember all thy
offerings, and accept thy burnt sacrifice; Selah. Grant thee
according to thine own heart, and fulfill all thy counsel.
—PSALM 20:1–4

I. Troubles are our opportunities to meet God

Humans seek God through troubles and think about the Lord the
Creator as we look back at ourselves. Therefore, troubles give us the
time to observe ourselves and can serve as a shortcut to God. In our
troubles, when we come before Him and call unto Him, He will in the
midst of His distinct purpose intervene in order to deliver us. In the
Bible, it is stated that when we are going through troubles we must
call out to God through prayer, and He will answer us (Psalm 50:15).

II. He answers in the Temple (Most Holy Place)

Abraham, our father of faith, while he was traveling and living in
the tents, always built an altar to burn offerings to God. Hence, he
was able to hear our Jehovah God's voice (Genesis 12:7–9; 13:4, 18).
God loves when we build an altar at church. There are many accounts
of prayers being answered while praying at church. The first thing
Jesus did when He arrived in Jerusalem was to enter into the temple
(Mark 11:11). Hannah received answer to her prayers while praying at
the temple (1 Samuel 1:9–10). The prophet Isaiah witnessed our God

seated on the throne in his vision while he prayed at the temple (Isaiah 6:1). Samuel also heard the voice of God in the temple since he was a young child (1 Samuel 3:3–4).

Holiness and sacredness are the essential conditions of the church.

III. Through prayer God will accomplish His will

When God gives us something, He does so for a reason. One labors and receives compensations upon completion of the work. In the same way, God desires us to receive the answer He holds in His hands, to be claimed by us through prayer. Our prayer should be sincere. God wants us to receive answers to our prayers more than we do. Prayer can be thought of as a spiritual labor, for which come answers to our prayers. Prayer is not a burden. When we depend on the Lord, it is said, "He will hear him from his holy heaven with the saving strength of his right hand" (Psalm 20:6). Therefore, we must always give praise to the name of our God, and be filled with confidence. Our Lord receives glory and honor through our prayers. Hallelujah.

DAY TWO

And it shall come to pass afterward, that I will pour out my
spirit upon all flesh; and your sons and your daughters shall
prophesy, your old men shall dream dreams, your young
men shall see visions: And also upon the servants and upon
the handmaids in those days will I pour out my spirit.
                                                    —JOEL 2:28–29

Pastor Kim, Yong-Doo: I preached a detailed message on an extraordinary vision that may appear during prayer, how a scheming devil may attack, and about a method of distinguishing between a devil and Jesus. We sang praises for two hours, and the sermon itself took another three hours. It was after one in the morning when we started the spiritual combat during our prayer. With the Holy Spirit's special intervention, it was as if we were on fire as we prayed. Even though it ended after seven that morning, we felt we did not have enough.

LEE, YOO-KYUNG MEETS JESUS FOR THE FIRST TIME AND VISITS HEAVEN

Lee, Yoo-Kyung: Pastor Kim's sermon talked about methods of chasing the devil away, as well as the possibility of Jesus' visit, so I deeply yearned and with all my might called out to the Lord, "Jesus, Jesus, I love You. Let me see You. Appear to me." I shouted and prayed diligently in tongues. About an hour had passed when suddenly a bright light shone, and someone was standing inside the light. I opened my eyes and was filled with shock, but did not see anything. When I closed my eyes again, I could see clearly, but I kept my eyes closed. Jesus stood before me wearing a brightly glowing garment, and it seemed like He was calling my name.

"Yoo-Kyung, I love you." Jesus said these words, then drew closer to me and sat in front of me. I had only heard about Jesus, but through prayer I was able to meet Him. I could not believe it. The Jesus I saw close-up was so handsome. I don't think I ever saw anyone as beautiful as Him.

Jesus' hair was golden and He had a beautiful, big eyes. My eyes are small. Jesus gently stroked my hair and said again, "Yoo-Kyung, I love you." As Jesus repeated those words, I began to cry and my heart melted. Jesus extended His hands toward me, saying, "I want to show you what heaven is like," and as He took my hand, my body suddenly felt as light as cotton.

Jesus said, "Hold on to my hands tightly." As soon as those words were spoken, behind the podium where the cross was hung, the wall opened up and my body felt it was being sucked toward the opening. Then I started flying like a bird with the Lord. I was flying in the sky wearing a white, toga-like garment. I saw many stars and our planet Earth. It became more distant, only to become invisible later.

As I was flying with the Lord, holding His hand, there was a light shining so bright that I could not open my eyes. I thought, "This must be heaven." Then Jesus explained that we were in heaven. When we arrived, countless angels with wings welcomed us, and Jesus took me around, introducing me to many angels.

Jesus took me into a room where there were many books. Among them, a big golden book caught my eyes. I became curious. I asked Jesus if I could look at the book, and Jesus gave me His permission.

I only completed elementary school. I have so much deficiency that I am unable to correctly read Korean. When I was in school my friends and kids from the school constantly made fun of me. There were many words written in the golden book, but I could not read it well. But I really wanted to have this book, so I asked Jesus, "Would it be OK for You to give it to me?" Then Jesus replied, "Yoo-Kyung, this book is not something you can have just because you want it," and He graciously smiled at me. Jesus asked me, "Yoo-Kyung, are you happy to be visiting heaven?" and I quickly replied, "Yes, Jesus. Very, very happy." Jesus said, "Pray diligently, obey Pastor Kim, and attend church services well, then I will take you to visit heaven more often, so be zealous." With that He took my hand and said, "You had enough today, so let's go back now." As soon as He held my hand we were flying in the sky and reentered the church through the opening in the wall near the cross behind the podium.

I was so happy. I prayed diligently in tongues. After it was over I shared my testimony of meeting Jesus and visiting heaven. Everyone was envious of my experience.

Baek, Bong-Nyo Awakens her Spiritual Sight

Sister Baek, Bong-Nyo: When we pray in unison at The Lord's Church, we turn on only one emergency light, and each individual gathers near the podium, kneeling down on their cushion to pray. Pastor Kim was giving his sermon, and we went into praying in unison. Despite the freezing weather we had to take our outer garments off.

Next to me was pastor's wife, who was dancing, filled with the Holy Spirit. Her dance was smooth, like flowing water. It was completely captivating and beautiful. She said she had never taken any dance or ballet lessons, but she was glowing and dancing beautifully as the Holy Spirit led her. As I was watching pastor's wife, I sincerely wanted to dance like her.

I continued praying in tongues. Suddenly a glorious golden light shone, and there stood Jesus dressed in a shining white garment, calling out my name: "Bong-Nyo. I love you." The Lord's warm and comforting voice stirred my soul. Words could not describe the overflowing joy of meeting the Lord.

I asked questions about heaven and hell, faith, and other concerns, and He answered them promptly. The Lord waited, counting the days for today to come. He was looking for a church for me to attend and came across Pastor Kim, Yong-Doo and his wife, Kang, Hyun-Ja, praying all night. He was deeply moved and at that moment decided to send me their way.

Even though I have been attending church for merely two months, I obediently follow Pastor's guidance. I asked the Lord again, "Lord, why have You come to meet with someone like me, and so personally?" He answered, "You have accepted the gospel my servant shared." Also, the Lord told me I would be used as an instrument to evangelize and many will be saved. He prophesied there will be a great revival in The Lord's church.

I thought silently, "How can I be used in that way with so much sin in my life?" Then the Lord, already knowing all my thoughts, replied, "Do not worry. I am with you." After the prayer rally, I shared my meeting with Jesus with pastor and his wife, and they shouted with great excitement, "Hallelujah." Pastor Kim said Jesus told him to document the matters of heaven and hell as they are revealed and publish the document as a book. He wanted me to confirm that with Jesus one more time, and I agreed.

Blessing services, burning prayers, and the dreamy meeting with the Lord. Some time had passed and morning came, but I could not wait until the next prayer service. I wanted to meet the Lord once again.

THE HOLY SPIRIT GUIDED BURNING PRAYER TIME

Kim, Joseph: I was calling out to the Lord during the unity prayer time as my body started to heat up. At the bottom of my right foot there are about fifty warts, and I had not walked properly since the previous summer. I went to see the dermatologist with my mother, and I was told to receive three treatments to freeze my foot and surgically dig out all the warts. There were no guarantees that this would cure my wart problems. I was very scared. I thought, "I am a freshman in high school now. I need to attend after-school tutoring and study extra hard, but what am I going to do? We don't have the money for the surgery."

My mother asked me to pray about whether to have the surgery. Therefore, I decided to attend the prayer rally, praying faithfully and knowing that God would heal me. I stopped attending all my after-school programs and concentrated on requesting earnestly for God's healing. My voice was second loudest in our church, next to the pastor with the resounding roar. Using this to my advantage, I delivered a burning prayer to Jesus. It was painful to kneel because of my foot, but I had to challenge myself if I wanted to receive His healing.

Kim, Joo-Eun: Everyone was praying out aloud with all their might. Pastor preached in his sermon that in order to meet the Lord, there is no other way but to pray out loud and with sincerity. I am in the sixth grade and am the youngest member of my family, but I sincerely prayed to meet with Jesus. While praying in tongues, I peeked to see if there were anyone who was able to meet Jesus.

Lee, Haak-Sung: First, I replayed the sermon in my head and concentrated on praying in tongues, as pastor instructed us to do. Without my knowledge, my prayer was filled with authority as my voice turned powerful. My body was burning up like a fire, and I had to take my outer garments off. Later, my shirt was drenched in sweat. I have never in my life experienced this blazing fire of the Holy Spirit coming over me. I was joyful and happy to pray. So, I prayed on bended knee and with painful paralysis, my legs went numb. Pastor Kim massaged my legs with his hands and relieved my paralysis.

Oh, Jong-Suk: After signing a debt guarantor document for my friend, which went terribly wrong, without a place to go my older brother kicked me out of the house. In the freezing winter, where was I supposed to go? I was sleeping around the nearby parks, starving and shivering uncontrollably, when I met Pastor Kim, Yong-Doo. He was the pastor of a church that an acquaintance of mine from work was attending. As I was wandering the streets, by chance I met Hee-Young, and through him I met Pastor Kim. For two weeks I ate and slept at the pastor's residence, and there I was trained spiritually and was able to attend the prayer rally.

With a loud shout of "Lord, Lord," we started our prayer rally, and soon it seemed the room was being filled with fog. In the fog I saw someone moving about. In an instant, I grabbed on to His ankle, and it felt like I was flying somewhere. I was in shock, so I opened my eyes. I started to pray again, and this time the person led me to a large, brightly shining place. It felt like I was in a world of lights.

It was like a dream. I had not been attending the church for that long, but for the first time I prayed and called to God on my knees with my arms held high. After the prayer service I inquired about my encounter to the pastor. He taught me that it was Jesus who appeared to me and that I briefly visited heaven, so when I pray diligently He will show me more amazing parts of heaven next time. I had never experienced anything like that before. We prayed on our knees, and therefore my legs were numb and in pain. But, my experience was fantastic.

Pastor's wife, Kang, Hyun-Ja: I hadn't prayed a decent prayer for a long time, so I was feeling the urge. Pastor decided not to go to the prayer mountain in the new year, but instead wanted to have a determination prayer rally at our church. I was so happy. Since many other members joined in the prayer, the Holy Spirit's intensity was so much more powerful. While praying, if an unusual spiritual environment arose, the Lord dealt with the pastor and each member individually with fiery authority. The spiritual dance that Mrs. Choo Thomas was anointed with, I yearned to receive. And later, for the first time I was able to dance the holy dance without hesitation.

For a while I hid this gift, and it was suffocating me as I danced secretly, worrying what the congregation would perceive from my dancing. Thinking that they would look at me with a strange stare, I hesitated; but today I am liberated, as I gave myself completely to the Holy Spirit to guide my dancing. I can no longer run away from the guiding forces of the Holy Spirit. My body was anointed as with fire as my hands freely moved to the music as the Lord lead me. From my mouth flowed a powerful prayer in tongues, a prayer of repentance.

DAY THREE

Thus saith the LORD the maker thereof, the LORD that
formed it, to establish it; the LORD is his name; Call
unto me, and I will answer thee, and show thee great
and mighty things, which thou knowest not.
—JEREMIAH 33:2–3

YOO-KYUNG PLEADS THE
DESIRES OF HER HEART TO JESUS

Lee, Yoo-Kyung: As usual, today after the sermon I prayed in tongues. Jesus called my name, "Yoo-Kyung." and appeared to me. I shouted out to Jesus, "Jesus, Jesus, Jesus, will You always appear to me?" Jesus replied with a smile, "Of course." I had a request for Jesus: "Jesus. Give us some financial help. We're having a hard time. My sister and brother are unemployed and are at home. Please make my mom well so she won't be sick anymore." So Jesus answered, "Yes, all right. Do you have any other requests?" I quickly said, "Pastor Kim, Yong-Doo is stressed out about his thinning hair, so allow his hair to grow abundantly." Jesus burst into laughter. He then replied, "He's on his own with that one," and looked away. Jesus was busy moving here and there meeting each praying individual.

DAY FOUR

Humble yourselves therefore under the mighty hand of God, that
he may exalt you in due time: Casting all your care upon him; for
he careth for you. Be sober, be vigilant; because your adversary
the devil, as a roaring lion, walketh about, seeking whom he may
devour: Whom resist steadfast in the faith, knowing that the same
afflictions are accomplished in your brethren that are in the world.
—1 PETER 5:6–9

YOO-KYUNG MEETS A DEVIL DRESSED IN WHITE

Lee, Yoo-Kyung: During his sermon today, Pastor urged us to be
alert during prayer. He said that if we were scared and unsure at any
time to call out to Jesus. When we see these horribly wicked demons
approaching us, we must relentlessly drive away the demons in the
name of Jesus and shout out for His precious blood.

Without a doubt, as I was praying out with all my might and with
a sudden burst of energy, I saw a devil that looked as though it came
out of a movie. Wearing a white garment and with long hair, it came
toward me dancing and speaking in a dreary voice, "Hahahahaha.
Hehehehe." In that instant my body was paralyzed with fear. Suddenly
I remembered pastor's sermon, and I started shouting, "You wicked
and cursed devil. I command you in the name of Jesus to flee from
me." But the devil approached closer to me crying "Hehehehe" and
opened its mouth to speak. Its mouth was so hideous it sent a chill
down my spine. At both the top and the bottom on each side of its
mouth was a sharp cuspid, and surrounding its mouth was blood. The
devil replied, "Why should I flee? Not only am I here to hinder you

from praying, but I will give you a physical ailment." It continuously surrounded me.

Precisely at that moment, I don't know how Pastor Kim knew, but he laid his hand on my head and prayed, shouting, "You filthy devil. I command you in the name of Jesus Christ to flee."

The devil was gone.

I was terrified. Pastor always told us, "Jesus is always with us, so we dodn't have to worry. If we stay fearful, it will return. So don't worry and be confident when we pray." I resumed praying, calling out Jesus' name: "Jesus, help me. Help me." I was calling out to Him for quite some time when Jesus appeared in the bright light. He spoke to me, "Yoo-Kyung, do not worry. I will protect you." Jesus comforted me with a pat on my back and said, "Yoo-Kyung. No matter what kind of demons attack you, do not be afraid and do not worry. With all your strength call out to me and I will come and cast the demons away. So, don't be afraid and be strong." I was comforted with by His words.

When I could not pray out loud or fell asleep while praying, the demons always took the opportunity to attack. This is the reason why pastor always trained us to pray on our knees, holding our hands straight up, and with a correct posture. At first this was hard, but now with God's grace we can pray two to three hours easily.

DAY FIVE

Then shall the kingdom of heaven be likened unto ten virgins,
which took their lamps, and went forth to meet the bridegroom.

—MATTHEW 25:1

WEDDING OF JESUS AND
SISTER BAEK, BONG-NYO

Author's note: The marriage between Sister Baek, Bong-Nyo and
Jesus symbolizes the relationship between the Savior and the sinners
He saved. He wanted to show this to the new convert, Sister Baek.

> Let us be glad and rejoice, and give honour to him: for the
> marriage of the Lamb is come, and his wife hath made herself
> ready.
>
> —REVELATION 19:7

Baek, Bong-Nyo: Pastor gave a fiery, Spirit-filled sermon on five wise
and five foolish brides. After service I started diligently praying in
tongues when the Lord appeared to me and said, "Bong-Nyo, let's go to
heaven." He held my hand and guided me. Soon I was standing at the
foot of our heavenly Father's holy throne. Jesus explained passionately
the reason why I was brought to heaven: "Bong-Nyo, I wish to have
a beautiful wedding in heaven with you today, and that's why we are
here." As soon as that was said, the angels started preparing my gown
and adorned me with many jewels. I have never seen anything like
the golden gown prepared for me. I was filled with joy and was beside
myself. I could only go along with what the angels were doing. I asked
myself, "Have I have ever experienced a proper wedding before?" I was

so overwhelmed with deep emotion. I was experiencing overflowing happiness, of which I had never dreamt, nor can I now explain.

Many angels and citizens of heaven congratulated our matrimony, and I shall never forget this scene. Right then the holy throne of our heavenly Father seemed to sway ever so slightly back and forth. Each time His holy throne moved, because God was so pleased, five brilliant colors radiated throughout. After the ceremony, I traveled holding the Lord's hand all over heaven. I was at the peak of my happiness.

LEE, HAAK-SUNG MEETS HIS MATERNAL GRANDMOTHER IN HELL

Lee, Haak-Sung: During the sermon, Pastor Kim mentioned, "There is a person who will visit hell today. Do not be afraid, but trust in Jesus. No matter what Jesus shows you in hell, do no worry." He continued with a proclamation, "Let us all pray earnestly to Jesus so we can see the miserable scene that is going on in hell."

With a firm determination, I started praying in tongues, when suddenly the cross hanging behind the podium radiated with bright light, and a round door appeared. A little later, Jesus appeared holding two lambs on His arms. Then the lambs disappeared as Jesus drew closer to me, gently calling out my name. "Haak-Sung. I love you."

This was my first meeting with Jesus, whom I had only heard about. Suddenly I was filled with excitement, and my body started burning. I could not contain the happiness that overwhelmed me. Jesus was wearing a radiating white garment. He spoke softly to me, "Haak-Sung, there is some place you have to go with Me, so let's go." I curiously asked, "Where are we going?" Jesus replied without revealing the destination, "You will know when you get there." As soon as Jesus took my hand, my body floated in the air as light as a feather, and my arms stretched out in front of me. Then in a blink of an eye I was dressed in a white garment, and it seemed we were being drawn into the door behind the podium. I was already flying up in the sky with Jesus.

In the distance I could see the Earth and its surrounding

atmosphere. After passing by, there were the cosmos, where the stars embroidered the night sky. Then we passed the galaxy, and after that came total darkness. A sudden fear struck me, so I held tightly on to Jesus's hand. Jesus led me, saying, "Let's go a little bit farther." When we arrived, there was a strange stench, and it was very dirty. I could hardly breathe due to the offensive smell all around me.

"Jesus, my beloved Jesus. Where are we? I can't see too well in front of me," I shouted, but Jesus said, "Haak-Sung, don't be frightened. This is hell. I will protect you, so do not worry. But look closely."

The fire heated the gates of hell bright red, and even before entering it was unbearably hot. I had to turn away from the scorching fire and the intense heat. I asked, "Jesus, how can we step into this pit of fire? I don't think I can do this." If I can try to make a comparison, it looked like a scene from a television program where an iron manufacturing company was melting and synthesizing metals for harbor building materials. The heat at the entrance to hell was worse than the hollow smelting pit on TV. It was a much more intense heat.

Jesus extended His hand and said, "Hold on tight to my hand," and the unbearable, burning heat dissipated. But it was so hot that I could still sense the intensity of the heat surrounding me. Where I went with Jesus was pitch dark, and I could not see a thing. It felt like I was in a room. Then, as soon as Jesus touched my eyes, I could see ever so clearly. There was an old lady with a look of despair sitting motionless and wearing a white traditional Korean dress. Jesus instructed, "Haak-Sung, look closer," so I walked closer to the old lady. It was my maternal grandmother, who had passed away a few years earlier.

When my mother left home, my maternal grandmother took in Yoo-Kyung, Yoo-Me, and I, and raised us. My grandmother loved us. It was not right that my grandmother was in hell. With astonishment I shouted out to her, "Grandma, it's me, Haak-Sung. How can a gentle and kind person end up here? Hurry, come out of there." My grandmother quickly recognized me, and surprised, she asked, "Haak-Sung, why are you here? How did you come here?" I replied, "Jesus brought me here. Grandma, hurry and come out of there." My grandmother cried and shouted, "Haak-Sung, as much as I want to get out, you can't do what you want here. You must not end up here. Leave immediately."

In tears I pleaded with Jesus, "Jesus, please help my grandmother come out. My grandmother lived a sad life." In an instant, a large snake appeared below my grandmother's leg and started coiling and winding up her body. I screamed loudly, "Ahh." My grandmother fearfully shouted, "Save me, please," but there was no use.

"Jesus, my beloved Jesus, I am the one who's done so much evil," I cried. "Please do something, please." Jesus did not say a word, but His heart was breaking as He watched. I cried and cried as I begged, but there was no use. Even in the midst of the craziness, she asked about the welfare of the family and worried about them. "Haak-Sung, how are your sisters? What about your mother?" I replied, "Everyone is doing well," and as I was answering her, the snake wrapped around her tighter. My grandmother's agonizing screams grew louder and louder.

"Oh, no. Grandma, I don't know what to do." I could not stop crying. Jesus took my hand and guided me, saying, "Haak-Sung, it's time to go now." I left the cries of my grandmother behind me and came out of hell. Jesus stated, "In hell, compared to the physical world, all your senses are more certainly and clearly alive." I remember that our pastor had mentioned this as well.

Visits to hell, which I had only heard about otherwise, were frightfully shocking, to say the least. With so many terrifying scenes and the disgusting stench, I could not stay there, not even for a brief moment. When I arrived at church, I thought about my grandmother and sobbed. Jesus reminded me to make a wise decision by saying, "Haak-Sung, don't cry. You saw it clearly, so go and serve the Lord faithfully. Do you understand?"

HAAK-SUNG'S FIRST VISIT TO HEAVEN

Jesus called to me, "Haak-Sung. Hell was gruesome, right? I want to show you heaven today." In a short time, we were in heaven. Groups of angels and many people who arrived in heaven before me came out to welcome me. The surrounding angels and Jesus joined hands to joyfully dance together. Everything about heaven was a complete contrast to the scenes of hell. In heaven, what I saw looked novel, amazing, and unbelievable.

While in heaven I made a request to Jesus. "Jesus, pastor's son, Joseph—his foot is covered with painful warts and he can hardly walk. Please heal him. And my mom is suffering with back pain. Help her not to be in pain. Help brother Oh, Jong-Suk, who is living in the church office, to quickly find a job. And lastly, help us to have a revival at our church." Jesus happily replied, "Yes, all right." Jesus looked at me and said, "Haak-Sung, that's enough for today. Let's go." When Jesus held my hand, we flew though the sky, arriving back at church.

I resumed praying diligently. I could not stop thinking about my maternal grandmother who is suffering in hell, and I burst into tears. I was in so much distress and pain, I cried out kicking and screaming, "Lord, what am I going to do? My grandmother died because of me. This pains my heart so bad. Grandmother. My poor grandmother." I cried until exhaustion. Then I started again. I called out to the Lord. I rarely cry, but I could not believe the tears that flowed for two hours, three hours, and then four hours. The first prayer session finished, but still I could not contain my sorrow.

I shared my testimony of visiting heaven and hell with others. Then at five in the morning we started our second prayer service, which ended five hours later. While pastor was giving his sermon, I saw Jesus. Just then, pastor's sermon became more powerful. Angels came down from heaven, lining up beside the podium, and some carried a bowl with a support. They captured and carried with them every prayer, praising, and singing, "Amen. Amen."

Even after all the services ended later that morning, I could not stop thinking about and agonizing over my grandmother, who was in hell.

DAY SIX

Thus saith the LORD the maker thereof, the LORD that formed it, to establish it; the LORD is his name; Call unto me, and I will answer thee, and show thee great and mighty things, which thou knowest not.

—JEREMIAH 33:2–3

NINE SHEEP

Baek, Bong-Nyo: Four hours had passed since pastor started his sermon. He was spewing out the holy fire onto us. There were nine members, but when excluding his family, there were only five church members left. Having a group of beginning believers did not hinder him, but he preached courageously and brilliantly. He held the microphone in his hand and walked back and forth as he preached. Not one of us batted our eyelashes, and even though it was already 2:00 in the morning, we all responded with, "Amen." The five-year-old Meena was also listening intently to the sermon.

As I fixed my eyes on the pastor, Jesus appeared with a throng of angels through the door on the cross. After some time I heard cries of various animals, then Jesus guided nine sheep with Him. "What is going on here?" I thought to myself. "These are real creatures." Among the sheep there were four smaller ones, and the one at the end was a lamb. Their white and curly fur was so pretty. I realized the number of the sheep Jesus brought and the number of the prayer rally attendees were in accord.

Yoo-Kyung, Joseph, Joo-Eun, and Meena are young, but even amongst the youngsters, Meena is merely five years old. I thought it was amazing that the number was in accord, and Jesus said, "You are all My sheep. I am always watching over you, so do not worry."

> Then said Jesus unto them again, Verily, verily, I say unto you, I am the door of the sheep . . . . I am the door: by me if any man enter in, he shall be saved, and shall go in and out, and find pasture.
> —John 10:7, 9

The nine sheep knelt down before Jesus. Meanwhile, Pastor Kim's sermon was burning up, and he spoke with the holy fire. In my mind I was concerned, thinking, "Pastor's lower back is constantly giving him pain. I hope he doesn't work himself to death." While I was thinking, Jesus abruptly got up from sitting next to the sheep and started touching Pastor Kim's lower back. Jesus was deeply involved in pastor's sermon, and shouted with glee, "Great job, Pastor Kim. You are doing great." Jesus walked alongside pastor with a constant, beaming smile.

Pastor exclaimed rapidly and loudly over and over again. Each time was filled and delivered with the blazing holy fire. When pastor moved to his left, Jesus moved left; when he moved to the right, Jesus also moved right. Then ten angels appeared. Among them, two stood right of the platform, two on the left, and on the wall where the cross hung, another angel stood with an open book recording something in a hurry. The rest of the angels surrounded the pastor carrying their bowls, collecting the sermon. When one filled the bowl, the next angel filled theirs, and this continued as they carried it up to heaven. Jesus rejoiced, and the angels also rejoiced. A few days before, I could only see Jesus while I prayed. But my spiritual sight is undoubtedly awakened, as I can see the Lord with my eyes opened.

After the sermon, it was finally time to pray in unison. As we prayed, the nine members of the prayer team all looked like we were fighting a battle. As we cried out to the Lord with repentance, the tears and sweat came pouring forth. During this cold winter weather, we shut the heater off as we prayed.

Then Jesus drew near, calling my name. The Lord spoke by comparing various churches, "Bong-Nyo, many churches sleep and have their red crosses lit up during weeknights, but the members of The Lord's Church pray so diligently. I am so delightfully happy now." He smiled. Then through the door on the cross behind the pulpit, angels descended in groups of three. Their wings were pulled back with one foot extended in front, and the other foot was slightly bent down as they approached. I was in awe and began counting them.

One, two, three, four, five; I counted for a while, but I could not see the end of their procession, so I stopped. They continued down endlessly and stood in front of the altar where the nine of us prayed. They took our prayers in the golden bowls and took them up and returned. The scene reminded me of when people lined up with water buckets during a drought waiting for the emergency relief truck; and upon seeing it, how delighted they are to receive water in their buckets.

The angels take prayers back to God. But lately, with the members of The Lord's Church worshiping all night long and without excuses throwing ourselves into prayer, the angels thanked us for giving them so much to do. They were so happy they did not know what to do.

A SPECIAL MEETING WITH THE TRINITY

Jesus looked as if He had come back from visiting somewhere. I asked, "Jesus, where did You come from?" Jesus explained, "With your diligent calling out to the Lord and worshiping day and night, the heavenly Father, Myself, and the Holy Spirit have marveled at your dedication. It is rare to find a church such as yours on Earth."

The heavenly Father asked us, "What can I give you?" He questioned Jesus, "My Son, what do You think I should do?" Jesus replied, "Father, do as You will." The Holy Spirit anointed us with the holy fire, oil, and heavenly gifts. The Father said, "For pastor's wife, Kang, Hyun-Ja, I especially want to anoint her with the blazing fire of the Holy Spirit and ability to heal the sick, and I want her to dance the spiritual dance with boldness."

The Gift of Spiritual Dancing Received

When pastor's wife started spiritually dancing, everyone watched in awe. Her face started to turn red as she danced with the Holy Spirit's guidance.

God abruptly pushed me into a place that seemed as if I were under water, as if my body and feet moved with a mind of their own. I could not think straight. A little later I heard the Lord's voice from somewhere say, "I will baptize you with the blazing fire." I felt as if I had been thrown into the oil, and my body instantly felt like a fireball.

Pastor's wife was behind the right of the pulpit, and I was on the left, burning like a fireball. We both moved our bodies naturally as the Holy Spirit guided us. I suffered with constant back pain for a long time and was almost at a point of being bedridden. I was taking medications for the daily pain it was causing me, but when I was filled with the power of the Holy Spirit, my pain was no longer present. Also, when I am speaking with Jesus, I do not have the pain. Even when I dance with all my might, my back still feels fine.

The Holy Spirit threw me into the fire once again. My mouth dried out, and I was so thirsty that I kept drinking water. My throat was dried and my lips blistered all over. Near me, pastor's wife was experiencing the power of the Holy Spirit as I did. Pastor Kim was praying with his arms high. Jesus walked toward me and once again taught me to be focused on God. After the prayer service, I shared the message.

Jesus suddenly started talking about the church and its pastors of Korea. With an angry tone He spoke, but I did not know why He was talking about it. He said, "What good is a church if it's only big and hollow with its cross lighting up? I chose the pastoral leaders to save the lost souls, but they lack prayer, and it's breaking My heart." As I listened, I urgently made a request to the Lord, "Lord, take me to see hell." Jesus replied, "Don't worry. Your son, Haak-Sung, went to hell and saw his grandmother there."

"Haak-Sung got to see his grandmother, but why can't I go? I miss my mother," I cried. Jesus continued, "If you went to see your mother in hell right now your heart would surely break, and when you witness the painful scene it will shock you. I will show you heaven first to erase your other thoughts."

SISTER BAEK, BONG-NYO'S HOUSE IN HEAVEN

I was dancing the holy dance and praying in tongues when Jesus held my hand, saying, "Bong-Nyo, come with me to heaven." At the instant I held Jesus' hand I was wearing a white garment, and we entered the door near the cross behind the pulpit. As soon as we entered I was flying with Jesus into the air like a bird. As I got higher, the Earth became smaller and smaller.

The universe was such a beautiful scene. We flew for a while, then we reached the galaxy. When we passed the galaxy, it became dark again, and I saw two roads up ahead. We went through the right road, so I asked, "Lord. Where does the left road lead to?" He replied that it was leading to hell. It seemed we were on the road for a while, when suddenly a light appeared that was so intense I could not open my eyes. Heaven was filled with stars. People on Earth often say the word *paradise*, but what I saw at that moment cannot be described with earthly vocabulary. "How can it be? How can this possibly be?" I asked. Humans cannot fully imagine what heaven is like.

Many angels greeted and welcomed me. Jesus said, "You've decided and committed yourself to diligently attending the church, so I want to show you your house in heaven. Follow me." I followed Jesus. I saw that many angels were involved in the construction of something. Jesus told me, "This is your house." I looked, but there was no house. I only saw a deep foundation as the angels used gold to conduct their work.

Jesus was saying, "In a few days your house will be going up. Don't be discouraged, but pray diligently and live faithfully. You worshiped the devil, and you have led many people into delusion. But, you made a determination to believe in Me and diligently attend the church." I answered Him, "Lord, thank You. Thank You so very much." I bowed my head, expressing my gratitude.

Jesus said, "I have a place I want to show you, so follow Me," and He lead me to another place.

Pastor Kim and his Wife's Treasure Storehouse and Their House

Jesus tenderly held my hand, "My beloved Bong-Nyo, I will show you the treasure storehouse and house of the people responsible for evangelizing to you, your church pastor, Kim, Yong-Doo, and his wife, Kang, Hyun-Ja. Watch carefully," Jesus explained. "The Earth's one thousand-story building is comparable to a one-story building in heaven, and everything in heaven is indescribable with the limited human vocabulary."

I walked holding Jesus' hand, and it seemed we were heading toward the center of heaven. Before my eyes an enormously large building stood tall, and the radiating light was so intense I could not lift my head. "Lord, the light is so bright I can't hardly see. Why is it happening?" I asked. Jesus replied, "This is Pastor Kim, Yong-Doo's house." Jesus lifted His right hand up and suddenly I could see clearly what I could not just a moment earlier, Pastor's beautiful new house in heaven. Then the Lord said, "Now, let's see Pastor Kim's treasure storehouse." As I was walking with Jesus, I realized that the distance from the house to the storehouse was about three to four bus stops in our earthly description. Pastor's treasure storehouse was heavily guarded with hundreds of angels, so we could not enter. When Jesus appeared, the guarding angels suspended their wings downward and stood upright and bowed before Him. Every treasure storehouse in heaven required Jesus' permission to enter them.

The radiant colors pouring out from the storehouse was an image to be marveled at. "Wow, Pastor Kim will be so happy," I said. Inside the treasure storehouse there were countless angels busy with amassing all of pastor's materials coming up from the earth. Pastor's treasures keep on accumulating. I asked Jesus, "Why is Pastor Kim's house so big, and why has he so much treasure?" The Lord answered me, "Pastor Kim,

Yong-Doo started his faithful walk early on, and he always prayed and served Me diligently."

Our pastor and his wife often argue, but Pastor Kim will quickly resolve the dispute and will go to church to repent. Jesus wanted pastor and his wife to stop arguing, and He told me to deliver this message to them.

Jesus said, "That's all the time we have today, so let's see more next time you're here." He brought me back to church. Jesus said one last thing before He left me: "When I died on the cross, many believed that I would not live again. They stopped believing me, stopped going to church, and now are doing other, worldly things." Jesus promised, "I cannot show you all of heaven at once, but when you pray diligently I will always bring you back so that you can see."

Pastor Kim, Yong-Doo: After hearing the testimony of Sister Baek, Bong-Nyo of our family's awards in heaven, Joseph and Joo-Eun started chanting. Also, their usual arguments subsided on their own, and they were busy building up treasures in heaven. Every praying team member was filled with joy and desired the blessings of our Lord.

SECOND PRAYER SERVICE: YOO-KYUNG MEETS HER MATERNAL GRANDMOTHER AGAIN IN HELL

> And from the days of John the Baptist until now the kingdom of heaven suffereth violence, and the violent take it by force. For all the prophets and the law prophesied until John.
> —MATTHEW 11:12–13

Lee, Yoo-Kyung: I was praying in tongues for thirty minutes when Jesus came to me. Jesus always wears lustrous white garments. Jesus took my hand saying, "Yoo-Kyung. I have somewhere to take you." So I replied, "Yes. I like being with You, Jesus." Soon we were flying in the sky. Jesus said, "Yoo-Kyung, listen well to what I'm saying. We are heading to hell right now. Do not be frightened. You just have to hold on tightly to My hand. I will be right by your side, so don't worry. I will protect you. I have someone to show you, so watch carefully."

As soon as we arrived in hell, I could smell some strange burning odors. The smell of a corpse made me nauseous. It was so dark that I could not see anything. Jesus shook His hand, and slowly the area started to light up. There was a dark room divided into different sections. My eyes met an old woman sitting and crying, and I realized it was none other than my maternal grandmother. My grandmother raised our family. I cried out when I saw her.

"Grandmother! What are you doing here? Why are you here? Please come out from this dark and empty room," I exploded with a loud cry. "Grandma, I really missed you. Grandma, I love you." My grandmother cried, saying, "Oh, my dear granddaughter, Yoo-Kyung. What are you doing here? I missed you so much, too." No sooner than when we exchanged these words I stretched out my hand toward her, and she also wanted to touch my hand.

Just then, Jesus stood by me and pulled me away so that I could not touch her hand. "Yoo-Kyung, you cannot touch her hand. Don't touch it," and He pulled me away. My grandmother and I both cried. "Grandma, I really missed you so much," I told her. Then she replied, "Yes, my dear, I missed you the most. But, how did you get here?"

"Grandma, I believe in Jesus. My church is having a special prayer rally right now, and I met Jesus. He brought me here." My grandmother cried and said, "That's great. You must be happy." I continued, "Grandma, my brother could not come with me today. He disrespected you, made you starve, and that's why you died." When I said that, she replied, "You're right, Haak-Sung, that terrible boy refused to feed me, and when he was hungry he only fed himself." Then she told me, "Regretfully, I am in hell. I want to go to heaven right now if I can, but since I cannot, I'm gnashing my teeth. Your maternal uncle's wife cursed me all the time, saying, 'When is that old hag going to die? Why is it taking so long for her to die?' Every day she cursed me, and when I had the infection, she did not get medical treatment for me. Instead, she stuffed tissue papers into my infected area, letting me die that way. That's why I'm still cursing her here in hell." She spoke words filled with hatred. A large snake coiled around my grandmother wrapped her so tightly she could not move.

"Jesus, please save her," I prayed. "Have mercy on my grandmother." Jesus spoke to me as I cried, "Yoo-Kyung, don't cry. This won't do. Let's go now." And with that, we left hell. Then he said, "I will dry your tears away, so hold on to my hands tightly." As soon as I grasped His hand, we were flying through the sky.

The sky in heaven cannot be described in words. That is how beautiful it is, with various beautiful shades of color. How can I describe heaven? Jesus tried hard to lighten up my sorrowful mood. I danced with Jesus in heaven for quite some time. Jesus and the angels gathered around dancing together in what looked similar to the Korean circle dance.

Also, in heaven, Jesus asked me to sing a song, and I sang a song I learned at church: "Praise the Lord, Oh My Soul." I sang it repeatedly when Jesus said, "Yoo-Kyung, let's stop here today and go back. I will bring you back next time." He then told me, "When you pray diligently, I will meet you and bring you back to heaven." With that, He commanded an angel to bring me back to church.

When I arrived in church, I began to cry while I prayed. I was seeing my poor grandmother suffering in hell, so I cried endlessly. After the prayer meeting, I confided in Pastor Kim, "Pastor, my maternal grandmother is in hell. What am I going to do? It pains me so deeply. She could have lived longer. My grandmother was so kind. She bought me tasty treats, and she was so tender to me. My grandmother raised us like our mother when we had no mom, but she is in hell. Pastor, I don't know what to do. I will never miss attending church. I will obey you no matter what." I wept loudly.

Pastor replied, crying, "Yes, I know you will." People sitting next to me listened and cried together as they rededicated their own faith.

DAY SEVEN

And he spake a parable unto them to this end, that men ought
always to pray, and not to faint; Saying, There was in a city
a judge, which feared not God, neither regarded man...
—Luke 18:1–2

Joo-Eun Awakens her Spiritual Sight

Kim, Joo-Eun: My friends Yoo-Kyung and Haak-Sung are enjoying
their prayer life after having their spiritual sights awakened, and I
was very envious of them. I prayed earnestly to awaken my spiritual
sight. I prayed in tongues for about an hour, when suddenly a bright
light shone. Then Jesus, wearing a white garment, appeared before
my eyes. Jesus had brown hair and was wearing a white, shimmering,
toga-like garment.

He called my name. "Joo-Eun, my beloved Joo-Eun, I love you." Jesus
drew closer as He spoke to me. I was surprised and said, "Are you really
Jesus? Wow, Jesus, I really love You. You are wonderful," and I shouted,
filled with excitement because I did not know what to do. Jesus sat in
front of me saying that He loved me. I ecstatically said, "Jesus, I really
love You," and He replied, "Yes, I love you very much as well." Jesus told
me, "Pray diligently, and I will reveal Myself to you. I will take you to
heaven and show you around. So, pray diligently," and He disappeared.

Seeing the Evil Spirits

When I did not see Jesus, I began to pray in tongues with all my
might. Suddenly, in front of me a strange object appeared, and it was

42

running toward me quickly. "Uh-oh. What is that?" I wondered. Both corners of its eyes wore slightly torn, and the right eye was like the starfish and had an X shape to it. This devil was covered with scars. I remembered pastor's sermon earlier about chasing out the demons in the name of Jesus, so I shouted, "In the name of Jesus, depart from me." The devil disappeared.

I continued praying, when something with eyes narrower than a cat's with a vertically lined pupil then appeared before me. It had wings like a bat, and when it opened its mouth there were sharp teeth protruding gruesomely from the top and the bottom. It rushed toward me with its mouth wide open to scare me, but I defeated it in the name of Jesus.

This time a somewhat familiar demon appeared, and I wondered where I had seen this one before. I realized it was the character I saw from the computer game *Starcraft*. This female demon ran to me. She tried to look intimidating by staring me down. A bit later she tried to look even scarier by letting her hair down.

Unlike other evil spirits who quickly fled when I mentioned the name of Jesus, this female demon did not go away so easily. Even after I repeatedly shouted it did not budge, and I was getting really scared. I rushed to Pastor Kim's side next to the pulpit and continued praying. Pastor took my hand and raised it up, praying with me, and only then did the devil leave.

YOO-KYUNG MEETS HER MATERNAL GRANDMOTHER AGAIN IN HELL

Lee, Yoo-Kyung: As I was praying in tongues, Jesus came to me. He said we had somewhere to go, so I followed Him. Jesus took me again to hell. Hell was so dark, and the flames were bright red. Someone called my name, "Yoo-Kyung." So I looked, and there was my grandmother. Surprised, I shouted, "Grandma, Grandma, why are you there? You were in a dark room before. Why are you there? Hurry and come out of there." At that moment, my grandmother's body melted away, and she transformed into a skull and skeleton. My grandmother's skeleton was still stretching out her hands shouting, "Yoo-Kyung. Ahh, it's so hot. Please save me. Ask the Lord to take me out of here. Please, I beg you."

I urgently asked Jesus, "Jesus, You love me. Please help my grandmother. Please?" and I stretched out my hand to try and hold my grandmother's skeleton hand. Jesus replied, "No, you can't. You cannot touch her," and blocked my way. Beside us was a large snake twisting its body and keeping watch. There were other smaller snakes piled up, also keeping watch over the people.

I was shivering with fear when Jesus held my hand tightly, reassuring me, "Yoo-Kyung, I am right beside you, so do not worry." The place where my grandmother was suffering was so horrendous. The water in the pot boiled up bright red, and in the midst of such torture she began resenting and cursing my maternal uncle's wife again. Then she said to me, "Yoo-Kyung, don't you ever come back to this place. You must go to heaven. I can't bear this heat. I want to die and do away with this torture. Ahh, it's so hot."

EXITING FROM HELL AND INTO HEAVEN

I left my grandmother's agonizing screams behind and left with Jesus. Then Jesus took me to heaven. In heaven, I danced in circles with the angels singing praises, and Jesus showed me many books. There was one quite large book, so I asked, "Jesus, what kind of book is this?" He didn't tell me, but said, "You should hold it." The book was so heavy I could not hold it properly.

The heaven's sky, the galaxy, outer space, and the stars in the universe were so beautiful. The skies of heaven were bigger than the galaxy or outer space and much more beautiful and radiant. Jesus said, "Let's stop the sightseeing for today and save it for next time." And, holding on to Jesus's hand, I returned to our church.

DAY EIGHT

Up, sanctify the people, and say, Sanctify yourselves
against to morrow: for thus saith the LORD God of
Israel, There is an accursed thing in the midst of thee, O
Israel: thou canst not stand before thine enemies, until
ye take away the accursed thing from among you.

—JOSHUA 7:13

SATAN'S TEST

Pastor Kim, Yong-Doo: It had been about a week since we started
the determination prayer rally. Our spiritual battle intensified, and
our physical trials continued daily. One by one, each of the prayer
warrior's spiritual sight opened up and they were filled with the Spirit.
Demonic forces then made an aggressive offensive movement.

Many personal situations arose, testing our anger threshold. On the
first day one of the tires on my car had a terrible tear along the side
below the hubcap. It was a difficult repair job, but the next day the
front tire had another big tear on its right side.

It looked as though someone had purposely done the damage.
When this happened, it was only two months prior that I had replaced
my worn-out tire with a brand new tire, and I was so frustrated with
the situation. Nevertheless, I did not complain to God, but instead I
shouted "Hallelujah" as I prayed with a thankful heart. Then the next
morning as I arrived at the parking lot, a tow truck took my car away.
This really was close to pushing me over the edge, but my wife and my
congregation members reminded me, "Pastor, you have to persevere
through this."

I went to pick up my car from the towing garage and with a smile said, "You guys sure are early birds. Do you work so diligently even in the early mornings? I am very impressed." With those words, I turned around and came back home. I babbled to myself under my breath, saying, "Wow, Pastor Kim. What's gotten into you? You did not get angry but instead suppressed it. You are really becoming a decent human being," and I laughed out loud.

When I got back home, I prayed, "Lord, if these are the things that the devil is doing, please help me be victorious and triumph until the end." The next day, someone had broken the car's brake lights, and then the day after that someone scraped the side of the car with a sharp object from one end to the other. I had nothing else to say but, "Oh, Lord," and endured these tests daily.

Kim, Joo-Eun: During the Sunday morning unity prayer service, I sat on a piano chair with my eyes closed. I prayed out loud when I saw a dark shadow. When I opened my eyes, I could not see the evil spirits, but when my eyes were closed, so many had appeared before me. When the demons disappeared, Jesus appeared in a bright light. As soon as He appeared, a sweet smell pierced my nose with a fragrant aroma words cannot express. I wanted the evening service to come soon so I could pray.

HOLY SPIRIT LED AN
INFORMAL AND RELAXED SERVICE

Pastor Kim, Yong-Doo: Sister Baek, Bong-Nyo; Lee, Haak-Sung; Lee, Woo-Kyung; and Kim, Joo-Eun were continually visited by Jesus as He concentrated on showing them to both heaven and hell. Following the awakening of their spiritual sight, speaking in tongues was followed by gifts of prophesying, knowledge, wisdom, and faith. Also, healing powers and casting out demons emerged little by little.

The church service progressed the way the Holy Spirit led. Until then the title in the church bulletin read, "The Holy Spirit-filled climatic hour," but it was replaced with, "A real Holy Spirit-led service." The worship, prayer, sermon, and offering formalities were removed, and we relied on the guidance of the Holy Spirit to lead and proceed with worship, prayer, and sermon proclamation.

The Sunday morning service started at 11:00 in the morning and ended in the afternoon at 1:30 pm. The sermon can run behind schedule, and since there are no first or second services there is no pressure to finish within a timeframe. Thus, the sermon can be delivered freely. The members who pray all-night vigils frequently complained the Sunday service alone did not fill their spiritual appetite. This was inevitable for these prayer warriors who start their prayer regimen every night around 9:00 or 10:00 p.m. and continue until the next morning. They are completely immersed with praise, the sermon, and prayer. I believe their faith exceeded those members who only attended Sunday service. This difference in the growth of their faith posed a serious concern.

In every process, from services and prayer rallies, Jesus attended and observed the content of each sermon, praise, prayer, and each believer's attitude. Each prayer warrior sees Jesus' presence during our all-night prayer vigils, so they do not feel tired, even though the service goes on until the next morning. We are always alert, and there is no time to let down our guard since the devil attacks without ceasing.

THE SUNDAY NIGHT SERVICE (ACTS 2:17–21)

Kim, Joo-Eun: I was praying in tongues when Jesus approached me saying, "Joo-Eun, I love you." He continued, "Joo-Eun, pray diligently, and I will take your hand and lead you to heaven. Pray without ceasing. I will show you heaven. Do you understand?" He said those words and went over to the pulpit where Pastor Kim was preaching.

DEVILS TAKING TURNS ATTACKING AND DISTRACTING US WHILE WE PRAYED

The devils appeared in groups because Jesus was not with us. One appeared flapping its wings like a bat with two small horns on the

47

head and eyes like a cat. Inside each eye was another sharp horn. That devil flew toward me with its mouth wide open, and inside the mouth were sharp teeth like Dracula's. Its nails and toenails were so sharp, it looked as if anything it touched would be sliced dead. The eyes were bloodshot. With sticky slime oozing from its mouth, it wanted to swallow me whole. I shouted, "In the name of Jesus, I command you filthy and dirty devil: flee from me." With that, it disappeared.

A little while later, a blue-faced devil with eyes the size of a fist approached me. Even though I was scared and had goose bumps all over my body, I screamed out, "In the name of Jesus, flee from me." But this devil did not budge. Instead, it continued to glare at me. I screamed out loud and was filled with fear when Sister Baek, Bong-Nyo, who was sitting beside me, joined in shouting, "In the name of Jesus, flee from us!" Only then did that devil flee.

I resumed praying when an enormous red dragon started flying toward me. Its eyes were green. Long, sharp horns protruded from its head. There were large, sharp teeth densely aligned in its mouth. There was smoke in its nostrils. This red dragon's canine teeth were especially terrifying. It lunged toward me as if it were about to swallow me alive. I did not budge. I stood my ground, praying diligently in tongues in the name of Jesus, and suddenly it fled. It was a most gratifying feeling. I did not realize the power and the magnitude of Jesus' name before this experience.

The next time, a hideous, terribly wicked, and skull-faced demon giggled in front of my face as though it were mocking me. In the middle of its skull, three horns stuck out as it continued to ridicule me. Once again I prayed in tongues using the name of Jesus to chase away the demon. I was thinking about Jesus hanging on the cross as I prayed when Jesus appeared, encouraging me and saying, "Joo-Eun, just a bit more, pray just a while longer."

HEAL THE WARTS ON THE BOTTOM OF MY FEET

Kim, Joseph: On the bottom of my feet there are about fifty warts, which prevent me from walking properly because the pain is so severe. I prayed diligently for Jesus to heal me, and I asked my friends Haak-Sung and Yoo-Kyung to pray for me as well. Pastor Kim also laid hands on my feet and prayed for me. My mother also prayed diligently for me. I realized that my own prayer is the most important, so I prayed strongly in tongues, calling out to our Lord.

Sister Baek, Bong-Nyo; Haak-Sung; Yoo-Kyung; and my sister, Joo-Eun, all met Jesus and received many heavenly gifts.

DAY NINE

And when the day of Pentecost was fully come, they were all with one accord in one place. And suddenly there came a sound from heaven as of a rushing mighty wind, and it filled all the house where they were sitting. And there appeared unto them cloven tongues like as of fire, and it sat upon each of them. And they were all filled with the Holy Ghost, and began to speak with other tongues, as the Spirit gave them utterance. And there were dwelling at Jerusalem Jews, devout men, out of every nation under heaven.

—ACTS 2:1–5

Lee, Haak-Sung: The devil's concentrated attacks began. The red dragon Joo-Eun told me about yesterday appeared before me. Its enormous size scared me. It had green eyes, and black smoke spewed out from its nostrils. Its teeth were sharp like horns, its claws pointed out, and the tail was frightfully long. Nevertheless, I prayed boldly, and it vanished.

A little while later a female devil appeared screaming, "Hee-hee-hee!" Her mouth was filled with teeth like a wolf's. Also, I began hearing an army marching in combat boots, stomping loudly behind me. Those images turned into dark shadows and surrounded me.

The devil's noise and the dark military boot stomps scared me, so I started crying, "Lord, help me. Please help me!" I was calling out to the Lord when He appeared in the light. The evil spirits vanished as soon as Jesus appeared. Jesus held my hand, and I sang and danced around and around with Him. I hesitantly said, "Jesus, I have something to say," and He permitted me to continue. "Pastor Kim is suffering with a severe back pain, so help him to get better. Also, my mom's back is not so good, so please help my mom not to be in so much pain. Also, Joseph and Joo-Eun stopped going to their tutoring classes to dedicate more time in prayer, so help them do well in school. Joseph's feet need healing, too," I added. And Jesus said, "Yes, my child."

LEE, HAAK-SUNG DEEPLY INDULGING HIS TRIP TO HEAVEN

Jesus called to me, "My dear Haak-Sung, do you want to visit heaven?" As soon as He took my hand, my body was dressed in a white gown. I floated in the air, and we flew toward the heavenly angels who awaited us. As we passed through the night sky, we arrived at the ever so radiant light before my eyes. I could not hold my head up properly in the presence of the brilliance. Heaven could only be described as a place filled with stars. I thought I was dreaming, but heaven was more real at that moment than the earthly world.

All of heaven was covered with gold from one end to the other. There was no place from which light did not emanate. Many angels and our saved heavenly brethren moved about busily. All the angels greeted me joyfully. I asked Jesus, "Jesus, I want to know if there's a house for me here." Then Jesus sent two angels to accompany me to where my house was. My house was not big, but the walls were made of golden bricks.

I saw an enormous flower garden, and I could not see where it began or ended. Various flowers filled the garden. As soon as I saw the garden, I had a sudden urge to jump in and roll around in it. As I smelled the sweet aroma of the flowers I was filled with joy and jumped up and down like a child.

I did not want to return to my world. I was feeling anxious because I did not want Jesus to say that I had to return. And sure enough, Jesus said to me, "Haak-Sung, we're out of time today, so let's get you back." I could not object to His firm voice, so I returned. I continued praying when I returned to church and until the prayer meeting ended. Afterward we ate rice balls and kimchee, which Pastor Kim's wife made. It was sweet as honey.

Jesus, Heal Our Wounds

Lee, Yoo-Kyung: I was praying in tongues when the devil approached me. There was a stitched up, X-shaped scar on its right eye and the left eye looked like a raccoon's black eye patch. It looked like a male devil, and I yelled out, "In the name of Jesus, flee from me." In an instant the devil fled. Then a skeleton demon appeared with three horns on its head, and the body was without any flesh. This demon also vanished in the name of Jesus, but yet another peculiar looking demon approached. The body of this third demon was covered with bat wings, and the nose was completely crocked to one side. With a dog tail and its broken wing, it flapped its wing as it attempted to start a conversation with me. It knelt down in front of me and complained, "What wrong did I ever do to you that you have to annoy me like this?" Its sharp claws came out to slice me. It pleaded, "Hey, I will never come again if you let me go inside you and come out just once." I replied, "You—you filthy devil. In the name of Jesus, get out of my sight!" With that, it vanished.

After that I fought off three or four more different demons, when suddenly I sensed a sweet-smelling aroma around me. Jesus came and called my name. Jesus said, "My dear Yoo-Kyung, give me your hand." So I extended my hands, and Jesus held my hands with His warm and gentle hands. I said, "Jesus, my shoulder is hurting badly," and as Jesus laid His hands upon my shoulders, the pain subsided.

Jesus' hand was a healing medicine. I made a request to Jesus, "Jesus, please go and allow Joo-Eun to meet You and hold her hands, too. Joo-Eun told me earlier that she wanted so badly to hold Your hand." At that point Jesus walked toward Joo-Eun and held her hands. He then turned to me saying, "My dear Yoo-Kyung, hold my hand." As soon as I grabbed His hand I was dressed in a gown, and we flew away as I sang praises holding Jesus's hand. Jesus encouraged me to keep singing, but I said to Jesus, "I am not a very good singer." But, Jesus kept insisting, so I reluctantly sang "Praise to Him, Oh My Soul." I sang it twice.

JESUS GIVES US NICKNAMES

Jesus gave each of the prayer warrior members of the church a nickname. It is great fun. Jesus called me "Speckle face" because I have many dots on my face. Joo-Eun's name is "Sesame" or "Freckles" because she is covered with freckles. Joo-Eun insisted, "Lord, why do You only give us girls nicknames and not our older brothers? Give them their nicknames, too." Then Jesus replied, "My dear Yoo-Kyung, Sesame, are you both happy?" I was feeling a little bad, so I replied, "No." Then Jesus answered, "Oh, really? I was just trying to make you laugh. Won't you smile?"

Then Jesus consoled me. He worried deeply for me, "My dear Yoo-Kyung, you cried so much after meeting your grandmother in hell." The Lord reminded me, "Yoo-Kyung, when I take you to visit hell, you must not lend your hand to anyone, even if it is your beloved grandmother. You must never hold anyone's hand in that place." He also told me, "I do not want to see you cry. Even though it's tough, always smile for Me."

I shared the nicknames Jesus gave each of us with Pastor Kim later, and since then without ceasing pastor calls us by our nicknames, even during his sermons. Every time this happens, we cannot contain the burst of laughter. Pastor Kim is so good at imitating each one of us. His sermon is so humorous and fun; he is like a comedian. My pastor is very funny. Even when he uses just a part of our nickname to call us, we simply reply boldly with an "Amen." "Round, Piggy, Sesame, Speckle," is what pastor will say, then the four of us will simply shout in unison, "Amen."

SISTER BAEK VISITS HELL

Sister Baek, Bong-Nyo: I was dancing the spiritual dance when Jesus came and tenderly took my hand. "My beloved Bong-Nyo," He said, "you have to come with Me somewhere. Let's go together." As soon as I held Jesus' hand, like before, I was flying through the night sky. I felt a sudden chill and became nervous. Jesus was aware of my nervousness and comforted me with His words, "Do not worry. I am right here beside you holding your hand, so be at peace."

Upon arriving in hell, I could not see anything in front of me, and I could smell the stench of rotting flesh. It turned my stomach. I could not see anything, but Jesus was walking and holding my hand. The only thing that calmed my nerves and gave me hope was the fact that I was holding on to Jesus's hand.

Jesus and I came to a very narrow road, and it seemed we were walking along a footpath between the spacious open rice fields in the countryside. The road was much too narrow for two people. I could not see the end of this road. On each side of the narrow road were steep cliffs thousands of feet deep. Even a little distraction would lead you to the fall to your demise. There were countless snakes piled up high on each side of the road and they looked intently at me.

Everything that was in this deep valley was in my visual field. I was so anxious and afraid. I called out, "Lord, I am so terrified." Then Jesus reassured me, "I am here with you, so do not be afraid." We moved forward when I turned to my right. The depth was so immense I was in shock. In that abyss I saw skulls and skeletons tangled together, all shouting out in agony. They cried out and pleaded loudly, "Save me!"

I put their cries behind me and walked on. This time there was an enormous dragon before my eyes. The dragon's size was immeasurable. Its torso was blue, and it had approximately fifty tails and forty to fifty legs. The face of the dragon was human, and there were forty to fifty heads. The teeth were terrifying, and the feet were webbed like a frog's. That lizard-like thing crawled about with horns prodding out from various areas of its head.

The tongue of the dragon extended from its mouth, catching and coiling around the people to throw them into the fire. This brutal and horrific scene was humanly impossible to imagine. Jesus told me, "Pay close attention," so I looked closer. I saw the second largest devil in hell coiling the people with its tongue and throwing them into the fire. One female among them caught my eye.

Meeting My Mother in Hell

I wondered to myself, "Who is that lady?" I was deep in thought as I watched, but when her eyes met mine, my body froze. It was none other than the person whom I missed and loved so dearly, my mother. I longed so badly to see her again. When I ran off, leaving my life behind, she took my place and raised my children. My mother's body was being wrapped up tightly by a demon. I screamed out to her as soon as I saw her. "Mom! Mom, why are you here?" At that moment my mother looked at me and shouted, "My dear daughter, Bong-Nyo, what are you doing here?"

Before she could finish her question, the second-highest ranking demon took my mother to a boiling hot pot of water and threw her in. The water was boiling endlessly, and when flesh was dropped in, the flesh, along with the bone, melted away. My mother was thrown in there and as she sank deeper she screamed out an agonizing cry, "Ahh! It's hot. Bong-Nyo, please ask the Lord to take me out of here. Save me please. I beg you." As she pleaded, the devil opened its other mouth, and with another tongue it coiled around my mother's mouth. The devil did not allow her eyes to sink. Instead, my mother was looking directly at me.

I screamed out to Jesus like a mad woman, "Jesus! My Jesus! Save my mother, please. I beg You. Lord, please save her." I cried and desperately begged Jesus, but He firmly answered, "No." I cried out again, "Jesus, I will take her place, so please let her out. She has no sin. I have so much more sin. Please!" Jesus said, "It is too late."

This is what Jesus said of my mother, "My dear Bong-Nyo, when your mother was living on Earth, if she had accepted Me, she would have been saved. I would have loved to bring her with Me to heaven, but she did not accept Me, nor did she have any faith. I cannot help her now." Once again, Jesus was heartbroken when He spoke. I could not bear the pain in my heart any longer.

Meeting My Father and
Younger Brother in Hell

Yet another familiar face appeared among the people tangled in the devil's tongue. I looked closely, only to find my deceased father and my twenty-six-year-old younger brother, who committed suicide by ingesting poison. Their eyes met mine. "My older sister, Bong-Nyo, how did you come here? This is not a place for you. Ouch. Please let me go. Let go." Hearing my brother's painful scream was paralyzing me. Both my brother and my father were naked. My brother pleaded with me as he was about to be thrown into the boiling water. "Big sis, pray to the Lord. Hurry and plead with Him to get me out. Help me to get to heaven. Now!" With his cry and plea, my brother was thrown into the pot of boiling water. I could hear the water boiling.

Since I was a young child, my father despised me, and that hatred magnified over the years. This father of mine also tried talking to me. "Bong-Nyo, when I was living I did so many despicable things that I regret so much now. I guess that's why I am here now. I am sincerely sorry. I was young, but my father especially did not receive any loving words or gestures from his father. If I did not get beat by him, I was lucky." I remembered all the things from the past and could not say anything to my father. I just watched him and cried. "Is he really my biological father?" I kept wondering to myself about my past. I could not deal with it.

I asked Jesus, "Lord, why did my father come here?" He replied, "Your father has sinned greatly. He did not believe in Me, but he also gambled without missing a day. When your mother was pregnant with your sibling and had merely one more month before the baby was to be born healthy and naturally, your father took that precious life in the womb by punching your mother in her stomach. The baby suffered trauma in the womb and died. Your father also forced you to bury a baby who was still alive up on a mountain. Don't you already know of this? After committing such wicked sin, he never confessed or asked for forgiveness. It is right that he belongs here in hell," Jesus said. His tone was filled with anger. As soon as Jesus finished His explanation, my father was thrown into the boiling water.

THE REQUEST OF MY IN-LAW IN HELL

I saw another face I knew, and it was my little sister's mother-in-law. My sister was recently married, and her mother-in-law was suffering with this same punishment. She earnestly requested that when I returned to Earth, she wanted her daughter-in-law and her family to believe in Jesus Christ, pray diligently, and see hell so that they would all go to heaven. Then she continued, saying, "I really didn't know there was a hell, or how hot and miserable it is here. I once held a title of deacon at church, but I never served at church. I had too many idols in the world, and it corrupted me. This is why I am here. I regret it so very much," she shouted.

> And cast ye the unprofitable servant into outer darkness: there shall be weeping and gnashing of teeth.
> —MATTHEW 25:30

My in-law was thrown into the hot water the same way. I was so scared and sad, I could not take it any longer. My face was covered with tears, and the burning odor made my breathing difficult. Every corner of hell was blocked off. I was feeling nauseous, and I just wanted to get out of there.

We were in front of a pit with an ample amount of space for about ten people to walk through, but inside there was something moving about. Approximately ten men and women were violently slicing at each other's flesh. There were maggots the size of a hulled millet seed going in and out of their eyes, nose, mouth, and ears. The eyes of the maggots glowed brightly. All kinds of bugs traveled in an out, tormenting them. Each time the bugs entered, the people cried out in agony as they violently jumped about. "Ahh! Stop! Please leave me alone."

I asked the Lord, "Lord, those bugs have shiny eyes, but do they ever die?" He reminded me, "It is written in the Bible, remember? Those maggots will never die" (Mark 9:48). While I was talking with Jesus, the maggots were gathered as tall as the height of a person, and I said, "Lord, it is so repulsive and scary. I want to leave quickly. I don't want to come back to hell anymore." Jesus replied, "I know, My child."

There was a gigantic iron pot where I went with Jesus. Inside the pot, some kind of liquid was boiling, but the boiling sound was very loud. Below the iron pot was an immense fire heating up the pot so intensely that the pot glowed bright red. In the pot were many bodies, but while I was looking I saw demons prepping my mother, brother, and in-law to be thrown in next. My mom's eyes and mine met once again. "Bong-Nyo, why are you here again? I told you never to return here, so why are you here? Do you like seeing your mother in agonizing pain? Hurry and leave," she said. My in-law was standing beside my mother shouting, "When you return to Earth, don't forget to tell my children to believe in Jesus and go to heaven. Please do this favor for me." Before she could finish her thoughts the demons angrily shouted, "What are you losers yapping about?" Then they lifted my mother and my in-law and threw them into the pot. Immediately my mom's and in-law's flesh melted off, leaving only the skeleton. They transformed into hideous, shapeless things. As I witnessed this horror, my body shivered with chills and I gnashed my teeth. I cried out, "Lord, please do something for my mother, won't You? Save her, please! I beg You." No matter how much I cried, begged, and clung to Him, Jesus only repeated, "It is too late."

I do not know if it was because I was endlessly crying, but Jesus continued shedding His tears. The Lord had an important lesson for me: "You have only one chance at heavenm, and that's while you're still physically alive." I could do nothing but helplessly watch my mother and my in-law.

As I watched my mother tortured, I flashed back to a time when my mother and I went to a restaurant to eat beef rib soup and potato soup together. I can no longer enjoy eating beef rib soup after seeing my mother in hell. When I see beef rib soup or potato soup in a restaurant, without fail I think of the scene I experienced in hell. Whether it is at home or elsewhere, when I see a bright red fire I am reminded of hell, and it saddens me. The fire in hell cannot be compared to fire in our physical world.

Jesus gestured to me to look on the other side, and there I saw a large black bowl. The living fire below the bowl heated the bowl so intensely the bowl changed from red to golden yellow. Many naked bodies shouted, "It's hot! I cannot stand this," as they jumped around inside the bowl. As they bumped into each other, they spewed out profanities. The scene reminded me of many people getting involved in arguments at the marketplace.

But once again my beloved little brother was at this location, and our eyes met. "Big sis, it is unbearably hot. Can't you save me? Please do something. Talk to the Lord and get me out of here. Don't you have pity for me?" No matter how much and how loudly my bother shouted, it was no use. My father was next to my brother, complaining. He did not attempt to talk to me this time. There was water boiling in the bowl, and that water filled the people up to their mouths.

I made an earnest inquiry to Jesus, "If You were not going to help my mother and brother out of hell, then why did You bring me here to endure this pain?" After a little while, He lifted my exhausted body up by my arms and led me out of hell. I said to Him, "Lord, from now on please do not bring me to see hell again." He brought me back safely to church.

A DEVIL DISGUISED AS JESUS

Lee, Yoo-Kyung: After praying until 7:30 the next morning, I came home hoping to get some sleep when I felt a presence in the room. I opened my eyes, but I did not see anything. When I closed my eyes again, Jesus we sitting beside me. A sudden fear came over me, and my body was covered with the goose bumps.

I prayed boldly in tongues. Suddenly, the person I thought was Jesus transformed into a dark demon, and it had dark blue eyes. As the demon rolled its eyes, it also raised its hands as it recited the Lord's

Prayer. It shouted, "All demons arise!" The demon did not leave, but sat between Haak-Sung and me. I was terrified, but Haak-Sung was asleep. I kept calm and braced myself, and with a commanding shout I said, "You devil, in the name of Jesus, flee from me." The demon instantly vanished.

DAY TEN

I say unto you, Though he will not rise and give him,
because he is his friend, yet because of his importu-
nity he will rise and give him as many as he needeth. And
I say unto you, Ask, and it shall be given you; seek, and
ye shall find; knock, and it shall be opened unto you.

—LUKE 11:8–9

IN THE NAME OF JESUS,
FLEE FROM ME, SATAN

Kim, Joo-Eun: While I was intensively praying in tongues, a red dragon appeared before me. As soon as I noticed the presence of the dragon, I was taken by surprise. The dragon suddenly dashed and leapt at me. The dragon had the eyes of a menacing crocodile with very thick and sharp claws, and he attempted to terrify me by thrusting his claws at me. The flaring nostrils emitted smoke that was disgusting and repulsive. I called out, "Satan, you hideous being, flee from me in the name of Jesus." I was shouting like a mad woman. As I shouted, the dragon turned and looked at me with evil, piercing eyes as he headed toward Brother Haak-Sung.

Perhaps Brother Haak-Sung noticed the appearance of the dragon and became startled. His praying in tongues became more intense and loud. Brother Haak-Sung shouted as I did, "Satan, flee from me in the name of Jesus." As Brother Haak-Sung shouted, the dragon approached me, and within seconds the red dragon transformed into a black dragon. With a wicked laugh, the dragon began to speak, "Do not pray. Why do you so effortlessly open your eyes when you pray?

If that is the case, then open your eyes. Why must you close your eyes during prayer? Open your eyes this instant. Why are you praying so intensely today?" The dragon trudged around me continuously as he spoke to break my concentration in prayers. Although I was frightened, I did not express it. I shouted again, "Hideous Satan, flee from me in the name of Jesus." However, the dragon did not heed so easily. Therefore, I had to emphasize Jesus' name more emphatically. With the shout of Jesus's name, the dragon once again turned to me with evil, piercing eyes, ground his teeth, and fled.

As I tried to regain my composure, I took a deep breath and started to slowly pray in tongues again. While I was praying, I noticed another form appear near me. The object was located in the corner of the room, and it appeared to be a white form or spirit. The strange form or spirit glared at me, and it began to advance toward me. As it came closer, I realized it was a popularized female spirit seen in many Korean horror movies and television. I became frightened and goose bumps ran down my arms. I recalled that I used to be frightened of this folktale ghost as I reminisced some of the movie scenes. However, as I continued to pray, I became courageous, and the fear faded away.

Nevertheless, there was still some remnant of fear in my heart. I knew if I expressed some fear, it would give the ghost confidence to vehemently attack me. With all my strength, I attempted not to express any fear as I fought the ghost with prayers.

From this experience, the hymn "Up and Fight Against the Devil" and the contemporary gospel song "Baptize with the Holy Spirit" have become theme songs of our prayer meetings for spiritual warfare.

I did not want the spirit to distract my prayers. I have to assume if many adults saw this figure, they would be very frightened of it. The purpose of this figure is to frighten people to death. Therefore, one should never express any fear toward it. Blood drips down at the ends of her mouth, and her hair appeared to be tangled and unkempt. She made an unholy sound like some hideous giggle. With all my strength, I shouted, "Flee from me in the name of Jesus." After I commanded it to flee, the spirit disappeared. I noticed tears streaming from my eyes.

I did not realize I was crying. However, the tears were tears of repentance from while I was praying. Then Jesus appeared, and in a lovely soft voice and with a smile, He called me by my nickname.

THE VISION OF JESUS CRUCIFIED

Jesus spoke to me, and soon after, hundreds of thousands of people appeared before my eyes. The Lord then stood among them and was silent. In my vision, among the people there were large buildings that appeared as castles. It appeared the people were demonstrating against something or someone. They were shouting and throwing objects toward Jesus.

I noticed some in the crowd throw hard objects at the Lord, but the Lord had His eyes closed and did not speak a word. I began to shout, "Why are you persecuting Jesus? Don't do that. Stop it." I became hysterical and ran toward the people and tried stopping them, but my attempts were futile. Moreover, I saw someone make a crown of thorns and then firmly press it onto the Lord's head. The blood gushed over His head, and His clothes were soaked with blood. There was so much blood it began to spill onto the floor. I saw the agony on the Lord's face as He tried to bear the pain. I felt so sorry for the Lord. I was not able to take it anymore. He was also whipped many times. As He walked up the hill of Golgotha, the Lord, with His broken body, fell many times. Each time the Lord fell, the Roman soldier flogged Him without mercy.

Although beaten down, the Lord lifted the cross and continued up the hill. Just as I remembered from the movies, a Roman centurion with feathers on his helmet began to beat on Jesus. The beatings were so profuse that He was not able to get back up. I could see on the top of the hill that there were three holes dug into the ground. The cross was placed over the holes. The holes were dug so that the nails could be hammered easily into the ground. Thereafter, they laid Jesus onto the cross. They began to hammer the nails into the Lord's hands and then into His feet.

The nail appeared thick and long. It was thirty to forty centimeters in length. When the nails were driven, the Lord yelled in agony. As I saw the nails hammered, I became so brokenhearted. I began to cry hysterically. The Lord made a faint sound and shivered, as He was in great pain.

The cross was lifted up. The two thieves being crucified next to Jesus began to lose their lives. Since the Lord lost so much blood, it seemed like He had no more blood to give. It was as though the ground were painted red with His blood. As I cried, the vision of His death disappeared and Jesus reappeared to me. He said, "My lovely daughter, Joo-Eun, pray relentlessly." I replied, "Yes, Jesus." I continued to cry and pray in tongues.

After a short time, it appeared that the Lord had come back. However, this time I sensed there was something wrong. I sensed uneasiness, and I felt frightened. I remembered my pastor telling me to be cautious since the devil can appear as an angel of light. I was told if I am not able to discern, I should either pray in tongues or test the angel by stating Scripture. I attempted to test the person by praying in tongues. The moment I prayed in tongues, what appeared as the Lord's face began to disfigure and turn black. The devil had come to me disguised as the Lord. The devil's eyes rolled in all directions and would not leave my presence as he tried to distract my prayers.

KANG, HYUN-JA'S PATERNAL AND MATERNAL GRANDMOTHERS IN HEAVEN

Sister Baek, Bong-Nyo: Our church has prayer meetings every night. Each night during my prayers, I think of my parents and brother, who are being tortured in hell. How am I able to forget and stop the pain from the thoughts that cross my mind? Today, as I was praying in tongues, the Lord Jesus came to me. I cried, "Lord, Lord." Jesus spoke and said, "Stop crying. I came to take you to heaven. Come with M." There was sympathy in the Lord's face as He held my hand.

Whenever I visit heaven I am awed at the mysteries, which are unlimited and eternal. I am awed at the wonderful sights. I feel that it would take forever to view and experience all of heaven. Jesus told me to go and observe the church in heaven. I asked Him, "There is a church in heaven?" He immediately replied, "Yes, go and see for yourself."

Just as He said, there was a church in heaven. As soon as we arrived, my jaw dropped, and we came upon a large and impressive building. I shouted, "Wow!" I was in a state of ecstasy. If one could see the magnitude of heaven's church compared to the largest church on Earth, it would not compare. It was so large. It appeared as though it could reach the sky in heaven.

As I arrived, it appeared as though worship services were ending. I observed two young adults exit the service. They appeared happy and were holding hands. Jesus guided me to the young adults and directed me to greet them. The Lord introduced us. The young adults replied, "We do not know you. Who are you?" Since they looked puzzled, the Lord introduced me once more and said, "Sister Baek, Bong-Nyo has just arrived from Earth. She is attending The Lord's Church in So Incheon. The pastor at her church is Kim, Yong-Doo. The pastor's wife is Kang, Hyun-Ja. Sister Baek, Bong-Nyo has been attending for two months." After Jesus formally introduced me, the young adults replied, "That's right, you are attending the church of my granddaughter's husband." They were so excited. Soon after, they asked, "What is the purpose of your visit?" I replied, "The pastor and his wife asked me to affirm that their grandmothers were in heaven." They were moved to realize that the husband and granddaughter were concerned about them.

The paternal grandmother began to give me an account of her life. "I died at the age of ninety-five. In that year, when I passed away, my son and my daughter-in-law told me that they would visit their son in America. I was living with my son, and I was too old to travel. Therefore, I had to move to my other child's home until the return of my son. However, my other child could not take me in, since they claimed that they could not afford it. I had nowhere to go. Soon after, my granddaughter's husband, Pastor Kim, Yong-Doo offered to accommodate me for fifteen days while my son was in America. This is how I ended up with them. I was an unbeliever. Since it was difficult for me to walk, Pastor Kim would carry me to church on his back each and every day. Pastor Kim would witness to me, and he stated that if I wanted to go to heaven with my granddaughter, I would have to accept Jesus Christ. I ended up accepting the Lord and Savior, Jesus Christ, and He had prepared a one-story home for me in heaven as my reward. I was an unbeliever all my life; however, I was very fortunate to get saved before my passing. This is how I got to heaven."

The grandmother asked me to pass a message of gratitude to her granddaughter's husband for the message of Jesus Christ.

Sister Kang, Hyun-Ja's maternal grandmother had a similar story of salvation. Both grandmothers expressed their concern for their sons since they were not saved. They hoped the message of Jesus Christ would be given to their children as soon as possible. They hoped their children would one day join them in heaven with the Lord. I could sense their apprehension from their voices.

Next, Jesus called to me and said, "Bong-Nyo, let us go visit the highest peak of heaven." When we reached the highest peak, I could see many areas of heaven. I could see many angels. I saw an enormous garden with many flowers of different varieties. It was impossible for me to count and imagine the many different kinds of plants and flowers. I could see the endless ocean, and it was clean and clear as crystal. There were many different beautiful ships floating on the water.

We arrived back on Earth at the church. After the Lord left, I began to pray in tongues once again. As I was praying in tongues, I was once again reminded of my parents and brother in hell. I cried for many hours. Tears continued to run down my cheeks, and I did not know what to do. Soon after, a group of fifteen angels appeared to me. As they drew near, I asked them what their purpose was in visiting me. They replied, "The Lord commanded us to go to the Earth and comfort Sister Baek, Bong-Nyo. This is why we are here." After they spoke, they circled around me and began to minister to me with warm words. As I was comforted, I was able to calm down, and my tears were wiped away.

The Visible and Non-visible Spiritual Awakening

As I continued to pray, suddenly I saw heaven open, and Father God was sitting on His heavenly throne. He spoke and told me to stop crying. The Holy Spirit came and whispered to me, "I will give you and Sister Kang, Hyun-Ja a gift of healing and the fire of the Holy Spirit. However, you must earnestly seek them."

As Jesus was standing next to the Father, He said to me, "Bong-Nyo, when you become weary and weak during prayers, I shall anoint you with the power of the Holy Spirit." I was comforted by His words. I asked the Lord about visible spiritual awakening, "Jesus, it has only been a couple months since I have accepted You as my Lord and Savior. However, by Your grace my spiritual awakening is alive. Why is it that the gift has been granted to me and not the pastor and his wife?" And Jesus replied, "Father God stated that it is not for them at this moment." I asked, "Why not?" The Lord replied, "Their ministry takes precedence, for the gift may become a distraction to their main function. Their main job is to look after the sheep and evangelize."

I could not comprehend the Lord's explanation. The Lord saw that I was puzzled. He already knew I would not understand. Therefore, He had to explain it in more depth. The Lord said, "Do not worry. There is both the visible and non-visible spiritual awakening. Soon, Sister Kang, Hyun-Ja will have visible spiritual awakening. She should patiently wait and not be anxious. Not having those gifts should not be a concern to you. It is My prerogative and My will that I give a visible spiritual awakening to the congregation and not to the pastor or his wife. The pastor and his wife pray without ceasing, and their faith is strong. However, the congregation is still young in faith, so I must strengthen their faith through spiritual awakening. Therefore, it is no one's concern how I distribute my gifts."

Congregation Delights in Shortened Service Time

In a harsh voice, Jesus stated that the churches and pastors are worshiping Him in vain. They follow tradition and the works of men. Many of the services are short and void in message. The length in worship and praise time has become unacceptable. They are more concerned with when it will be over. The preaching time has been shortened. Jesus was expressing His distress. Generally, services are about an hour in length; however, many services have become less than one hour. They are in a hurry to finish. Jesus would like to manifest in the preachers' bodies, but the pastors preach in the flesh and not in the spirit. They are more concerned about time management than preaching in the Spirit.

With less worship and service time, many preachers are utilizing the free time for personal use such as dining, taking trips with the congregation, and wasting time on other trivial matters. Some pastors are distracted and deluded with attractive sisters. They give more attention to the attractive sisters. Moreover, some pastors do not treat the congregation with equal respect. The wealthier members are given more time or respect than those without money. These types of pastors are not spending enough time in prayer for the glory of God, but they are praying trivially, which is frustrating and dismaying to our Lord. The messages are not led by the Holy Spirit. The messages are provided by the strength of the pastors' knowledge and their flesh. Messages not from the Spirit will result in short, vain preaching. Preachers elect not to be led by the Holy Spirit, but by the will of the congregation.

Jesus desires to powerfully anoint and utilize pastors for God's glory. However, the preachers have, by their own will, given up to seek the Lord's anointing. Now their carnal mind rules over their spirit. Many preachers cannot feel God's heart and desires. God is deeply saddened.

When expanding or building a church, some preachers do so for the sake of their own glory and pride. In their hearts, the building is a monument to themselves. These types of pastors spend very little time in prayer and are preoccupied with the materialism of the world.

As the Lord told me about these things, I saw the expression of grief on His face. Although many preachers can boast about their spectacular buildings, heaven considers it trivial. Heaven's way is higher than Earth's; what one perceives as important on Earth may be incidental in heaven.

Jesus told me, "Not all pastors are wicked; however, the disobedient ones must be disciplined. If they do not repent, I will throw them in hell. In hell they will be tormented, and in a short time, I shall take you there, where you will witness those who have gone before them." I was frightened when the Lord told me that we would visit hell once more.

The Lord's Diagnosis on Cults

Whenever I am curious about anything, I have an obsession to find the answers. I had a question about cults, so I decided to ask the Lord, "Jesus, before I was evangelized by Pastor Kim, Yong-Doo, I was a fortune teller and was into worshiping idols. However, the pastor paid special attention to my family and now we have all been baptized. I have learned about many things, such as the Trinity, heaven and hell, eternal life, and eternal death. Due to the pastor's persistent prayers, on the very first day I attended the church service I was baptized with the blazing fire of the Holy Spirit. With the baptism, I began to pray in tongues. When I told other believers from other churches, they would tell me that I was in a cult and they would gossip about what I had told them. They told me what I was experiencing was dangerous and that I should leave Pastor Kim's church. Therefore I asked the Lord to please explain to me what cults are.

There are some believers who have been Christians for decades, and they claim to be very faithful. These believers stated to me that when one dies, he or she enters either heaven or hell. They claimed that a person like me, or anyone else for that matter, could not visit heaven or hell while they are still alive. They said it was nonsense. The members from the other church attempted to persuade my daughter to attend their church. They said my church had issues on doctrine and beliefs. Furthermore, they would make sarcastic remarks about our prayer meetings and ridicule the lengthy hours. They claimed I must be in a cult since our prayer time is held from 7:00 a.m. to 8:00 p.m. They further claimed that Pastor Kim and the church might be a cult. I prayed, "Please Lord, what if our church is really a cult? What will happen to my family?"

The Lord asked, "What is a cult? People are criticizing and judging one another because of their differences, denominations, and doctrines. They are committing sin. However, I am very pleased with your church. You and your church members pray without ceasing throughout the night. Those who have persecuted you and called you a cult will know I live and am the Lord. You have received the gift of healing the sick and are able to cast out demons. You also live by following the Holy Spirit."

Jesus continued, "People who judge and criticize one another will receive terrible judgment. Do not let them lead you astray. I am deeply moved by your prayers. Do not worry. I will protect you and your church. Although it is My wish to reveal Myself to all My people and grant them spiritual gifts, they do not seek Me. Many are not praying according to My will."

The Lord's face expressed anguish. Hesitantly, I asked Him about our church, "Jesus, what will become of our church?" The Lord then spoke, "You are fortunate to be filled with the Holy Spirit and to receive the gift of tongues so soon. The holy fire will be felt and received by the congregation."

GOD POURS DOWN
ANOINTING OIL ON PASTOR KIM

During long services, Pastor Kim powerfully preaches through the strength of the Holy Spirit's anointing. Some might assume that we would dose off during long services; however, the assertive preaching, praising, singing, and fired-up worship are all done with so much compassion that we are full of energy and can continue all night through the next day. One day, our pastor preached with such assertiveness that his face turned red. During the sermon, which was powerful and passionate, I saw a vision of God's glorious throne. Father God was pouring down anointing oil. It appeared that the Holy Spirit was anointing the pastor with fire. I could see Father God continuously pouring down fire and anointing oil onto the pastor. The preaching became very powerful and delightful.

The pastor was imitating a rice mill. A rice mill separates the grains of rice from husks. I saw the Lord Jesus laughing with joy. The Lord told an angel to record the events of the service. The Lord told the angel who was recording the events to record it diligently. The angel acknowledged and obeyed.

COUNTERFEIT CHRISTIANITY

I had to ask a question to the Lord about another church, "There is a church that has many branches throughout the world and even in Korea. They also seem to have similar worship services and a cross at the altar. Some say that their numbers are great due to their history and tradition. However, it seems to me that they also believe in Jesus as we do. Are they believers like us?"

After I asked, Jesus answered, "If they believe in Me, of course they will be saved. But that church degrades the Word of God by wedding it with the world." As we were discussing the other church, the king of demons suddenly appeared. The evil one looked worried and appeared apprehensive of his plan with that particular church. He appeared very nervous and began to walk toward me.

THE KING OF DEMONS REVEALED

Jesus said, "Many of God's people are very ignorant of the devil and the evil spirits. My people faithfully live their lives without giving much consideration to the enemy; however, the devil will attempt to hinder your work. Be of good courage."

I went to visit the pastor's home later in the afternoon. When I arrived, the pastor was writing in his journal and noting what had happened during the night. He had had another spiritual experience during his all-night prayers. The pastor had first recorded his experience on tape and was now journaling on paper. As the pastor continued to journal his experiences, the pastor's wife and I knelt down to pray beside him. The Lord's presence was there to protect us from evil spirits.

As the pastor's wife and I were praying, an enormous red dragon appeared to us. The dragon was so large that we could only view the body and not the whole beast. This beast had entered through the front door and was standing next to the shoe rack. The height of the dragon appeared to be as high as the sky. The expression of the beast was pure anger. It kept wiggling its nose. I felt nauseous and dizzy as I became frightened. The dragon expanded it wings, which were shaped like a bat's. The tips of its wings displayed thorns shaped as sharp knives. As the dragon flapped its wings, the thorns would scatter down toward hell. The thorns would strike at the spirits in hell and the spirits agonized and cried in pain.

As I continued to pray, I became more frightened as I was shown a large chair. The side and height of the chair seemed endless. It was a rocking chair of some sort. The dragon spoke, "I am trying to enter your body. How dare you challenge me. I am the king of hell. All in hell obey me with fear. Who do you think you are? You are nobody. You do not have the right to reveal my identity."

As the dragon scolded, his expression of anger turned into an expression of realization. "Aha. I now know who you are. One of my subordinates has just informed me of you. I had previously ordered this subordinate to deceive and lead many people to hell. However, he came back unsuccessful. When I asked him why he had failed, he stated, 'My king, you must see for yourself why it is so difficult. I first thought I could easily lead people to suicide. However, the prayers of Christians are very powerful.' 'What are you stating?' I scolded the subordinate. I had to verify the subordinate's claim. It was true, it was nearly impossible to fight the prayers."

Although the dragon frightened and scolded us, we were safe

through Jesus' protection. The devil shouted vulgar profanity and said, "I have been hindered." Then Jesus replied to the beast, "Where do you think you are? Do not be rude and violent. If you touch one person from The Lord's Church, you will be punished and my Father will strike you." The beast was distressed, and he then suddenly vanished.

The Lord Jesus spoke and said, "That dragon in hell attempted to deceive you as the king of evil spirits. This is the first manifestation of that particular beast. He had always sent his subordinates to the Earth to do his bidding. Pray diligently and without ceasing. Always be cautious, and do not worry, because the triune God will always protect you."

EVANGELIZING WITH BOLDNESS AND FAITH

Pastor Kim, Yong-Doo: It was Tuesday evening and the temperature was seven degrees below zero. However, with wind chills, it felt like fifteen below zero. The wind was howling. When it brushed up against the skin, it felt like very sharp knives. Despite the weather conditions, Haak-Sung, Yoo-Kyung, Joseph, and Joo-Eun went out to evangelize.

Before the four would go out to evangelize, they would prepare themselves diligently by praying with the power of the Holy Spirit. The Lord would anoint them with holy fire. They also made sure they had warm clothes before they ventured out in the cold. One of the four youngsters had warts on the bottom of his feet and could not walk properly. However, he was very dedicated to evangelizing.

Although it was not mandatory to go evangelize in such harsh weather, the four were doing so out of appreciation of God's grace. The four discussed a game plan to evangelize more successfully and effectively. They knew a great reward awaited them for tirelessly doing the Lord's work. In the extreme cold weather, where one can even see the steam come out of his or her breath, the four went on their merry way to win souls for the Lord.

The four youngsters returned late. I thought they would be tired and taxed over the extreme cold weather. I thought the four would say that would be their last time. However, they were filled with joy and the

Holy Spirit. They were excited and could not wait to talk about their endeavor. One of the youngsters stated that they had met a brother who previously attended our church. He was a brother I persuaded daily to return to church. The brother never returned. When this brother met the four youngsters evangelizing on the streets, he gave them ten dollars so they could buy some soup at the local restaurant to warm up. Moreover, he was so impressed with their laboring that he stated he would return to church.

They also visited and evangelized at a local hospital. Another brother saw the four youngsters and gave them ten dollars as well. He was also impressed and said, "Thank you for your tireless effort under these extreme weather conditions." He had comforted them with his kind and encouraging words. The four youngsters said to me, "Pastor, we never realized that evangelizing would be so fun and enjoyable." The Lord was with the four youngsters as they evangelized all day.

These youngsters come from difficult backgrounds and circumstances. A couple of them are not physically healthy. However, in spite of all their disadvantages, they diligently attend prayer meetings. Furthermore, they are growing under God's grace.

That evening, the youngsters and the church continued with prayer meetings nightly. The youngsters decided to tithe the money they had received to the church as a thank-you offering to the Lord. The prayer night went into the next morning. They had visited heaven. They are now totally dedicated to the Lord, and they will never compromise on their faith or obedience. They are part of God's army.

DAY ELEVEN

And these signs shall follow them that believe; In my name shall
they cast out devils; they shall speak with new tongues; They shall
take up serpents; and if they drink any deadly thing, it shall not
hurt them; they shall lay hands on the sick, and they shall recover.
—MARK 16:17–18

Kim, Joseph: I have witnessed other members of the congregation visit
heaven and hell. I have witnessed them having conversations with the
Lord. I also desire to have a spiritual awakening. I pray diligently on
a daily basis, seeking the spiritual awakening. My heart yearns and
desires it every day.

I prayed for the spirit of repentance so that I could repent in tears.
But not a single tear could I produce. There are warts on the bottoms
of my feet, and they become more painful each day. It is becoming
more difficult to walk, for I cannot bear the pain. As I prayed for
healing, I suddenly felt the presence of the Holy Spirit, and my body
became hot as fire. Then I felt a presence in front of me. The presence was very bright. I felt someone touching my head and feet. After
my prayers, I asked Joo-Eun if she had noticed anything during my
prayers. She said, "Yes, Jesus was embracing you."

THE ENDLESS ATTACKS
BY THE EVIL SPIRITS

Kim, Joo-Eun: I was praying in tongues for about ten minutes when
an evil spirit appeared. The evil spirit had eyes that resembled a
crescent moon. The colors of its eyes were black and red. The hair

was unkempt and messy. The evil spirit giggled as it stared at me. I shouted, "We expelled the king of evil spirits from our house. What makes you think you are worthy to fight? An inferior, subordinate evil spirit is not much of a challenge. In the name of Jesus, depart from me." The evil spirit departed.

As I continued to pray, another evil spirit in the form of a dragon's eyes approached me. At first I was startled and frightened; however, I was able to calm myself down. I shouted, "You are not worthy of a challenge. Depart from me in the name of Jesus." It departed.

The electronic piano was playing a gospel song titled "Baptize with the Holy Spirit." It is a fast-paced song. As the song played, I raised my hands and sang with the music. I also prayed in tongues, and I felt the presence and the power of the Holy Spirit. I felt the holy fire on the bottoms of my feet work its way up to the top of my head. As the holy fire worked its way up, I could hear the fire roar. My body felt like a fireball. The room inside was cold and the heater had not been turned on, but I was burning up. I was also having difficult time breathing.

As I earnestly prayed, a bright light appeared before me, and in front of that light stood Jesus. He was calling my name. In a soft voice He called out, "Joo-Eun, I love you. Pray without ceasing, pray diligently, pray with all your heart. Do not stop." I sensed warmness and I was able to see Jesus more clearly.

Ah, then I knew why Jesus told me to raise my hands higher. I was able to see Jesus more vividly. I told Him, "Wow, I can see You more clearly, Lord. I love it, Jesus. Thank You." As I cheered, the back of my hair flew as though a wind was carrying it. I was feeling good. I stopped praying for a moment to enjoy my jubilation when an evil spirit appeared. The evil spirit had three heads with a horn on the side of each head. The evil spirit was blacker than darkness. The evil spirit wore a mask, and its wings were shaped like a bat's. It attempted to frighten me when it struck the ground. However, I shouted, "You are no challenge for me. In the name of Jesus, depart from me." Afterward, I continued to pray in tongues.

Lee, Haak-Sung: As the congregation was praying, I felt a lightning bolt strike me, and holy fire went through my body. The holy fire would heat the place. It would almost become unbearable if I had any warm clothes on. I used to wear a jacket and a vest. Now I wear a T-shirt to our prayer meetings.

As I got deep into my prayers, evil spirits began to appear one at a time. Then three evil spirits appeared at the same time. They all had unique characteristics. Whenever I used the Lord's name, the evil spirits fled. Then the Lord Jesus appeared and comforted me.

Lee, Yoo-Kyung: As I was praying in tongues, an evil spirit with long eyelashes appeared in front of me. It was crying. The evil spirit begged me to listen to what it had to say. "It is very cold. I am so cold. Is there any way you can make me warm? Please?" I replied, "You filthy evil spirit. In the name of Jesus, depart from me." Then another evil spirit appeared. It had large ears like a donkey with wings of a bat. It flapped its wings continuously. The evil spirit's eyes were bulging out like a frog's, and it had fangs like Dracula. Its body was covered with blood. It had long, sharp fingernails, and there were three fingers on each hand. The evil spirit tried to frighten me by thrusting its nails at me. I became very frightened and said, "Jesus, help me." Then I shouted, "You evil spirit, in the name of Jesus, disappear."

Soon after, another evil spirit appeared. It looked very ugly and weird; however, it only had one ear and only the whites of the eye. It was very scary. Goose bumps began to appear all over my body. I began to cry. Jesus and His angels appeared, and the evil spirit fled. Jesus then comforted me with His voice.

MEETING THE LORD IS ALWAYS GOOD AND FULL OF ANTICIPATION

The Lord was holding my hand, and He spoke to me in a gentle voice, "Yoo-Kyung, do not be frightened. I am always with you wherever you are; therefore, do not worry." He continued, "Why are you crying? Do not be intimidated by the evil spirits. I will protect you."

The Lord squeezed my hand and said that we should go to heaven together. After a while, Jesus drew closer and hugged me tightly. I was comforted and felt very warm in His bosom. I wanted to be with Jesus always and forever.

Jesus said for me to wait and that He would return shortly. He came back with a cute lamb. Its fur was curly. The baby lamb cried out, "Baa." The lamb's fur was very fluffy and nice.

Meeting the Lord is always wonderful. I am always full of anticipation. Jesus said, "Yoo-Kyung, now I must go back." I replied, "Jesus, I love You." I expressed my heart to Him. Jesus expressed His heart in return, "Yes, I love you as well." Then He took me back to the church.

The House of Jesus in Heaven

Baek Bong-Nyo: While I was intensely praying in tongues, Jesus came to me. He called out to me, "Bong-Nyo, do you want to go to heaven with Me?" Excitedly I replied, "Yes, Lord." One cannot possibly express the sight of heaven with human words. The Lord told me, "You cried so much as you witnessed your parents tormented in hell. Therefore, I took you to heaven to comfort you and wipe away your tears. Do not cry anymore. Be of good courage." I was very grateful and encouraged.

The Essence of God and the Trinity

As I was praying in tongues, I began to hear something magnificent. It was very loud. I could not ascertain where the music was coming from. Suddenly the Holy Spirit came to me from the vicinity where the Lord Jesus was standing. As the Holy Spirit appeared, it stood in front of the Father's throne. The Father's majesty and glory were so great, I could not lift my head. I bowed before Him. The essence of the Father is indescribable. His majesty is beyond great. I attempted to lift my head to get a glimpse of the Father, but the pure brightness of the light prevented me from seeing Him.

Father God is light, and a finite mind would not be able to

comprehend or imagine His glory. With that said, it appeared that the image of God resembled a man's. The magnitude of Father God appeared as though He covers the height and depth of heaven. His throne appeared as though it covers the ends of heaven from east to west. There seemed to be a formation of clouds hovering over Father God's throne. A luminous light brighter than the sun showered down.

I felt like a speck of dust as I stood before God. I thought to myself that the Holy Spirit is like a shadow, the way a shadow follows a person during the day. The Holy Spirit always looks misty and blurry to me. He is faster than the speed of light, appearing and disappearing instantly. He has a voice that is very soft and gentle. It was not my intention to look into His eyes, but I saw them.

It appeared as though the thoughts of the Godhead were in concert. Shortly after, the Lord said, "Bong-Nyo, let's go visit hell." He held His hand out to lead me. I was very apprehensive about going back to hell. The thought of seeing my parents frightened me very much. I resisted and said, "Hell is very scary. No, I do not want to go." The Lord replied, "Do not worry. I will not take you to see your parents." He said it gently with a smile.

SWARMING INSECTS IN HELL

The Lord and I arrived in hell. We were in front of a gigantic rock, the size of a mountain. The rock was covered with bushes of sharp thorns. There were swarms of poisonous insects and worms. I witnessed count-less people. It was impossible for me to fathom a precise number. The people were tied to the rock with their arms and hands spread out. At first, they all looked normal. They looked like normal human beings. However, their bodies deteriorated as the worms and poisonous insects gorged on their flesh until only their decrepit bones remained.

I have never witnessed these types of worms and insects. Some of the worms had white hairs on their bodies, like a caterpillar has. The eyes of the insects radiated like lightning. These horrendous insects were crawling and basically covered the rock. The mass of worms with white hairs on their bodies made the rock look like a white mountain. The number of insects and worms was infinite. They would bite into the peoples' skin. When the people moved, the insects would mercilessly tear into the skin. The people with all their effort attempted to be still and not move, but as the insects crawled up their bodies, their efforts were in vain. As the people became more agitated and the movement of their bodies increased, the worms would stick onto their flesh and their bites would penetrate into the bones.

People cursed and cried out as they skirmished. The more they skirmished and resisted, the more the worms devoured and feasted. The souls again attempted not to move, but it continued to be in vain. The insects tore into their flesh, devouring and chewing down to their bones. The people became decrepit skeletons. It was an ugly and horrific sight. I did not want to witness this carnage anymore. I begged the Lord, "This is too much for me. It is too repulsive. I do not want to see anymore. I wish to go somewhere else." The Lord then said, "Let us go visit one more place." He then took me to another place in hell.

We entered a dark tunnel. I was distressed because I could not see in the dark. I held the Lord's hand very firmly. I was very frightened. As we walked forward, small flashes of fire erupted in the air. There were people dressed in white. As the Lord and I walked by, their white dresses turned black.

We entered a cave with a black door. The Lord opened the door. I could hear people screaming. The noise and screaming were horrendously loud. The screams reminded me of animals howling in the night. It sounded like the cries of wolves and foxes. They cried out, "Oh! It is not fair. I'm in torment." Their cries became louder. It sounded like tigers growling.

I was startled and frightened. I could not go any further. As I stood in front of the black door, I noticed a demon standing guard. The demon spoke to me, "You have come all this way. Why do you not go in a little further? Go ahead, go inside the cave." I replied, "You are a demon. You demons only deceive and mislead people into sickness and pain. Then after you mislead them, they lose hope and end up fading away into darkness. I will not enter the cave." I looked to Jesus and said, "Jesus, I am very frightened. Please let us go from here." Jesus said, "Do not worry." The Lord waved His hands, and the demon became dust.

THE GANG OF DEMONS BLOCKING OUR PATH TO THE LORD'S CHURCH

Jesus said, "It is enough; let us leave this place." Jesus took me back to heaven, and when we arrived, He commanded one of the angels to escort me back to Earth. On our way to Earth a hoard of evil spirits chased us. The evil spirits were very ugly and frightening. Although the angel escorting me flew very fast, the evil spirits were just as fast. One looked like a dragon with wings on its back. There was also one resembling a snake and another with a frog's head. The last one had the head of a human, and he was laughing at me as he was chasing us. Then I saw the head of the human evil spirit split from the forehead down to the chin. As the head split, I noticed the face splitting in half to become a mouth. The lips were red, and it had teeth resembling a shark's. The mouth began to open and close constantly.

I was very frightened, so I asked the angel, "Can we go any faster?" The evil spirits were already ahead of us and blocking our way back to church. The other evil spirits that were behind us caught up as well and began blocking our way. They were all prepared to attack.

At that moment, I remembered a previous sermon from the pastor. The sermon discussed the war in the heavens with angels and evil spirits. While the angels delivered prayers to God's throne, the evil spirits tried to hinder and prevent them.

> Then said he unto me, Fear not, Daniel: for from the first day that thou didst set thine heart to understand, and to chasten thyself before thy God, thy words were heard, and I am come for thy words. But the prince of the kingdom of Persia withstood me one and twenty days: but, lo, Michael, one of the chief princes, came to help me; and I remained there with the kings of Persia.
> —DANIEL 10:12–13

The first evil spirit that blocked our path was the one with the human head. I was very frightened and startled as the evil spirit opened its mouth. The angel shouted with an urgent voice, "Lord, please come now." As soon as the angel shouted, the Lord appeared in front of us. With a mighty and powerful voice He rebuked the evil spirits: "How dare you try to attack My child. Be gone, now!" Within a second, the evil spirits disappeared.

OUR CHURCH AND THE CONGREGATION TURNED INTO A FIREBALL

When I arrived back to the church, I began to pray in tongues. The Holy Spirit swept through the congregation with holy fire. The weather was very cold. It was early morning, and the wind chill made it feel much colder.

The church building was very cold, and it was difficult for us to lift our hands in the air to pray. Our hands felt frozen. However, despite the conditions, we continued to pray. As we prayed, we began to sweat and our body temperature rose. We had to take off our thick jackets and coats. The Holy Spirit continuously anointed us with holy fire. The Holy Spirit's fire continuously flowed into my heart, head, arms, and the rest of my body. When we finished our prayer meeting, we noticed it was seven o'clock in the morning, and we had been praying for more than fourteen hours.

DAY TWELVE

When a strong man armed keepeth his palace, his goods are
in peace: But when a stronger than he shall come upon him,
and overcome him, he taketh from him all his armour wherein
he trusted, and divideth his spoils. He that is not with me is
against me: and he that gathereth not with me scattereth.

—LUKE 11:21–23

Pastor Kim, Yong-Doo: The four young teenagers, Joseph, Haak-Sung,
Yoo-Kyung, and Joo-Eun, left to evangelize despite the cold weather.
Joseph stated that he evangelized to a Buddhist monk. He told the
Buddhist monk, "Believe in Jesus Christ, then you will enter heaven.
If you continue to live your life as a Buddhist monk, you will go to
hell." After Joseph had spoken to the monk, the monk arrogantly
shouted, "You are a student of Korea. Do you not know your own
history? Christianity has only been established in Korea for about
one hundred years, but Buddhism has been in Korea for thousands
of years. Do not disrespect the ancestors." However, Joseph continued
with his evangelizing and preached, "Believe in Jesus Christ. He is the
only way to heaven. Please believe in Jesus and be saved." As Joseph
finished preaching, the monk replied with an angry voice, "Do you not
have any fear or respect? Go and educate yourself about the history
of Korea and Buddhism. Go and obtain the correct knowledge and
faith." The monk walked away in annoyance.

Joseph was a bit stubborn and continued to follow and evangelize the
monk. Although the monk denied Joseph's message, Joseph felt victorious with his mission. All four teenagers returned, and their hands

were red from the cold. The youngsters stated that they had evangelized for more than four hours, but they were not content with their mission. They had walked to many places and evangelized in markets, hospitals, and businesses. They continue to evangelize every day.

THE DEVIL COUNTERFEITED AS THE LORD'S ANGEL AND JESUS HIMSELF

Sister Baek, Bong-Nyo: I was praying in tongues, and thirty minutes into praying I saw five angels flying toward me. I decided to test the angels to determine if they were angels and not evil spirits. I continued to pray in tongues until they drew closer to me. As they drew closer, I saw the friendly smiles on their faces. The angels continued to smile and presented themselves as friends as I continued in my diligent prayer in tongues. I assumed that my diligent praying in tongues would confirm the angels as friends. However, within a short time, their white gowns turned black, and their angelic wings vanished. As they moved, their bodies would squirm and twist. I continued to vigorously pray in tongues, and they began to fall onto the church floor. The noise from their fall was very heavy. Truly, the spiritual gift of praying in tongues is powerful and great.

I had not imagined how praying in tongues could be so strong. I thought to myself, "What can I do to be effective for the kingdom of God?" I had only been a Christian for two months. I attempted to compose myself, but the evil spirits continued to appear in front of me. They resembled the monsters that are on television movies. There were several heinous-looking creatures, all more appalling than the other evil spirits I had seen before.

It did not matter how many there were; I cast them all out one by one in the name of Jesus Christ. They all fled. As I cast out the evil spirits, Jesus came and said, "Bong-Nyo, I am your Lord. Trust Me." However, His voice was eerie and His behavior was bizarre. The Lord had never said to me, "I am the Lord." Whenever He comes to me, Jesus comes gently and quietly. Within His presence, my heart becomes warm and

I am at peace. However, I was agitated and fearful this time. Moreover, I felt as though the hairs on my head had begun to rise. I thought to myself, "Oh, this must be an evil spirit counterfeiting as the Lord." With confidence, I shouted, "In the name of Jesus, depart from me."

As I commanded the evil spirit to flee, the spirit transformed into an hideous animal. I could not tell what type of animal it had changed into. I had never seen that type of animal. It had eyes within its eyes and they continued infinitely. The animal had hands shaped as a hook. It attempted to attack and scratch me with its hooks. As it thrust its hooks at me, I became frightened and shouted in Jesus's name several times. It resisted, but after several shouts it fled.

THE EVIL SPIRIT DISGUISED AS A BEAUTIFUL WOMAN

I could not have imagined the next appearance of an evil spirit. It was very attractive. I thought to myself, "How could such a woman look so beautiful?" This evil spirit was more beautiful than any woman in the world. She was very stylish and sophisticated. She was slender and had a beautiful figure. The woman wore a two-piece business suit. She walked as a natural model and gently approached me. She bowed to greet me and began to speak. She said, "How long have you been attending The Lord's Church?" I ignored the question and continued to pray in tongues. As I prayed, the evil spirit knelt down next to me.

Although she appeared very elegant and exquisite, my body had the goose bumps. As soon as it leaned over to me, its face split in half from the forehead down to the chin. The beautiful face turned into a horrible nightmare. Its lips split as well and the upper lips began to roll back and forth while the mouth opened and closed. I was astonished how the evil spirit was still able to speak even though its mouth was all torn up.

The evil spirit shouted, "Go ahead and continue to pray. It will not be easy. I will not withdraw." Within the split face were enormous teeth. The teeth were as sharp as a saw and the top and bottom teeth complimented each other. They looked like the ones I had observed yesterday. The distraction was not going to prevent me from praying. However, the evil spirit would not withdraw. I realized the Lord had come, and He then began to speak, "Bong-Nyo, do not stop praying. Pray zealously. I will rebuke and hinder the evil spirit." I therefore prayed more earnestly. Then suddenly, the evil spirit flew up into the air and transformed back into a beautiful lady. This time it was wearing a beautiful wedding gown with beautiful shoes designed with floral patterns. It looked gorgeous. The woman flew down to me, blinking its big, round eyes.

The Lord whispered into my ear and said, "Continue to pray and observe how the beautiful woman will transform back into an ugly spirit." I continued to pray zealously as the Lord commanded.

THE PASTOR'S ENJOYABLE SERMON

The pastor's sermons are very enjoyable and pleasant. Even though the preaching went on into the early morning, we felt as though it was not long enough. The pastor's preaching was powerful, robust, and enjoyable. The pastor stated, "Oh, it is getting very warm." The pastor said that as he continued to preach jumping up and down. Furthermore, the pastor was preaching with humor.

The pastor is a very talented person when it comes to imitating or impersonating someone. The pastor continued to belittle himself by saying, "I have lost all my hair due to a drought; even weeds could not grow on my head. My head is protruding and not very attractive. What am I to do?" The pastor made an expression of a crying face. Due to the pastor's funny gestures, we were all laughing out loud and falling from our seats.

Since the pastor was not spiritually awakened, he could not observe what was happening. The pastor became very happy and acted like a little child. Charmingly, he laughed, "Hee hee hee, my Lord, please pat my head as many times as You like so that I may not become a bald-headed man." As the pastor continued to preach, he was running side to side across the altar.

When the sermon concluded, we would begin our prayer meeting. During that night, in my prayer, the Lord came to me and said, "Bong-Nyo, let us go to heaven." He held my hands and we arrived in heaven. Although Jesus is in heaven, He is restless for saved and unsaved souls. All I can do to please Him is to be obedient by attending church, worship passionately, and pray unceasingly.

The Earth Revolving and Rotating, the Four Seasons, and the Changes in Weather

As I stood in front of the Father's throne with the Lord, I could see the light that was so radiant. Jesus meticulously explained to me the process of how Father God operated day and night and how the Earth rotates (Genesis 1:16–18). The Lord asked me to observe more carefully. I had many questions and a doubtful mind, but I was curious about what I had seen since my knowledge and mind was limited.

The Lord gave me a short and simple explanation of the Trinity. "Bong-Nyo, listen carefully. People on Earth cannot understand God's higher ways. They have limited ability. When the saints die on Earth and come to heaven, they will be given the capacity to fully understand. However, it is difficult for Me to explain so that you will perfectly understand. Just listen carefully to what I am describing to you."

Jesus continued to explain, "When the Father opens and closes His eyes, a tremendous, radiant light shines down on Earth to dictate the seasons of cold and hot. God is operating all of it (Psalm 74:17). Moreover, the Father plans all things within His will, and before He makes a decision, it is well thought-out. It was the Father who sent His Son, Jesus, to the Earth and become flesh, for Jesus to suffer and be crucified on the cross to save all mankind. Therefore, for whomever wants to come to the Father, the Son provides a door. The Holy Spirit is God's Spirit. He is always with us."

As Jesus was explaining, the Holy Spirit appeared and stood in front of me. I was having a conversation with the Holy Spirit when

Jesus said, "Let us go visit hell once more." As soon as He held my hand, we were already in the darkness of hell.

THE SINNERS IN THE RED LIGHT DISTRICT FACE BRUTALITY

The Lord had brought me to hell, but then He departed. Without Jesus, I was alone in hell. All of a sudden, fear overcame me, and I began to shake. I felt uneasy. It did not matter whether I was in hell or not. Without the Lord Jesus, I would feel uneasy anywhere. As I walked forward in fear, an enormous gray-colored mountain appeared within my view. There were no trees on the mountain. The mountain appeared to be some distance away. I could see pairs of stones or what appeared to be jars on the mountain. There were countless pairs of stones on the mountain.

My curiosity drew me closer to the mountain. As I stepped closer, I noticed they were not pairs of stones or jars, but people. Their bodies were covered with small white bugs. The bugs looked like sow bugs. Although the white bugs were on their bodies, the people did not make an effort to remove them. Then more of the white bugs began to climb onto their bodies and began penetrating their skin, nostrils, mouth, and ears. As the bugs penetrated the peoples' bodies, the people turned into ugly figures and they all became skeletons. One odd thing I noticed was that the bugs did not go into the peoples' eyes. As I drew closer to observe, I noticed the people in unspeakable pain.

I asked Jesus, "Lord, why are these people in such brutal torture?" Jesus said, "The women in this place are those who sold their bodies. The men are the ones who committed adultery with these women. Look closely once more," He said. I looked closer and I saw that their hands were bound (Revelation 22:15).

It was too hot. I was in agony. I could not stand it anymore. It was so hot I had to fan myself. However, when I fanned, I was fueling my own fire. I was then thrust in front of the Father's throne. I saw the Triune God gather in one place. The Father stated, "The human body is limited and frail. We cannot overload it with too much fire." Therefore, Jesus touched me, and I felt the temperature of my body cool down. The high temperature gave me a headache, but the Lord's touch quickly alleviated the pain.

COUNTLESS VISITS FROM THE DEVIL

Lee, Haak-Sung: While I was passionately praying in tongues, a huge dragon appeared. Joseph was praying next to me. The dragon was frightful and ugly. The dragon had three heads, with the middle head being larger than the other two. The dragon's body was very large, and it began to walk closer to me. It then began to thrust its claws.

The evil spirit I saw a couple of days earlier appeared again. The dragon drew my attention, and I became very frightened. I shouted, "In the name of Jesus, depart," and the evil spirits departed.

After I had cast the evil spirits out, the Lord Jesus appeared and called unto me, "Haak Sung, I love you. Your faith has grown much." Jesus then returned to heaven.

The evil spirits began to appear relentlessly. I began to pray in tongues with all my strength. Another dragon appeared, but this one was not the same as the others. This dragon had three heads as well, but the two smaller heads had the form of a snake. An evil spirit with the wings of a bat flew over. I was very frightened. I urgently called on the name of the Lord for assistance. "Jesus, please come help me," I shouted. Jesus appeared, holding a lamb. The Lord stated, "How dare you come here and bring chaos. Depart now." As soon as the Lord commanded, the evil spirits fled. The Lord watched over us as we continued in prayer.

The Lord drew close to me and said, "Haak-Sung, you and the other youngsters all went out to evangelize despite the cold weather. I am well pleased. In fact, my heart is well pleased because all four of you evangelized passionately and zealously." He was complimenting our efforts.

Kim, Joo-Eun: While I was praying, I saw in my vision the devil coming toward me from the corner of the prayer room. It was coming from my right side. The devil had a full body, but I could only distinguish the facial attributes. What was most vivid was its crescent moon-shaped eyes. I cast it out in the name of Jesus. As soon as it departed, a huge dragon appeared. The dragon had sharp claws with numerous heads attached to the body. There must have been at least a couple hundred heads. All the heads would open their mouths at the same time. As they opened their mouths, I saw the sharp, menacing teeth. They looked famished and ready to devour me.

Within that moment, I heard the gospel song "Baptize with the Holy Spirit." The song was from an electronic piano. The electronic piano was playing from its prerecorded program. As the song played, I danced with the rhythm and I shouted, "You filthy and ugly Satan. In the name of Jesus, depart from me." As I finished shouting, the dragon departed. However, another evil spirit took its place. This one looked very funny, and it made me laugh hysterically. The evil spirit had a small body with an enormous head. It was essentially a bobblehead. The large head contained many different-sized eyes. The eyes were aligned in a zigzag manner. The evil spirit possessed wings like an eagle folded against it body. As it walked, it tottered amusingly. I shouted in the name of Jesus; however, it did not depart. I shouted the command once more. After the third command in Jesus's name, it departed.

I continued to pray in tongues. After some time had passed, the Lord Jesus appeared and spoke, "Joo-Eun, I love you." He spoke with a soft and gentle voice. After I heard Jesus's words, my heart was delighted. I replied, "Jesus, I love You very much." I said it again, and I used my hands to form a heart to express my love. Jesus, in return, formed His hands into the shape of a heart. With laughter He said, "I love you, too." I asked, "Jesus, can You stay here with me? Please do not go. If You leave me, the evil spirits will return." The Lord agreed to stay with me.

As time passed, my prayer in tongues became intense. The Lord left as I continued to pray. As I was praying, I heard a disturbing sound. A group of evil spirits had appeared. I had never seen that type of spirit before. They did not have bodies; they were all shaped as an eye. There were different-sized eyes. Some were round eyes, some were in the form of a triangle, some were slanted eyes, and so forth. Even though they did not have mouths, they all began to speak.

As they stood in front of me, they all shouted, "Do not pray! We are going to distract you." They repeated the same statement over and over. I became frightened, and I was uncomfortable with their presence. Therefore, I shouted, "In the name of Jesus, depart from me." They were still present, and they began to make a weird noise. Within that moment, the Lord returned and said, "Joo-Eun, do not look or listen to anything except from Me." As the Lord spoke to me, He covered my ears with His hands. He said, "Joo-Eun, you can speak with Me." The evil spirits scattered at the presence of the Lord, and they soon departed.

Lee, Yoo-Kyung: While I was praying in tongues, an evil spirit with a bizarre hairstyle appeared. The evil spirit had no body; it was just a head with hair in the center. There was no hair on the side of the head, and the hair in the center was tied together with a string and made into a ponytail. The head spoke, "Do you want to dance with me?" I replied, "No, you filthy evil spirit. In the name of Jesus, depart from me." It departed. After some time had passed, another evil spirit with its two arms cut off appeared, and it danced toward me. The arms were severed from the shoulder and blood was hemorrhaging profusely.

The two dismembered arms moved from side to side, dancing in the air. It was a grotesque site. I shouted, "Depart in the name of Jesus," and the two arms departed.

I continued to pray intensely, and the Lord appeared. "Yoo-Kyung, do you want to visit heaven?" the Lord asked. With excitement, I replied, "Yes, Lord."

SWIMMING IN THE OCEAN OF HEAVEN

The galaxy is truly wonderful and beautiful. And as usual, the sky of heaven is awesome and marvelous. The sight is inexpressible. When we arrived in heaven, the Lord took me to a very high place. As the Lord and I laughed, an angel standing next to the Lord stared at my face. I asked the angel why he was starring at me in such a way. The angel answered, "I just wanted to get a closer look at you." We both ended up laughing.

Jesus told me, "Despite the cold weather, you have faithfully evangelized. I will give you a great reward." I replied, "I did not do anything worthy to receive a reward." But Jesus said, "No, you have done a great job." I rebutted, "No, Lord, evangelizing is my job. I do not deserve a reward for what I am called to do." The Lord was impressed with my response and said, "All right, thank you, Yoo-Kyung. The weather is very cold. Make sure you wear something warm when you go out to evangelize." With excitement, I answered, "Amen."

The Lord began to move my hand in a circular motion. I told the Lord I was becoming dizzy, and the Lord joyfully laughed. I began to joyfully laugh as well. The Lord then led me to the ocean of heaven. I jumped in joy and shouted, "Wow, there is an ocean in heaven, as on Earth. It is clear as crystal and vast. Lord, I can see through the waters."

With a smile on His face, the Lord spoke, "Yes, this is the famous crystal-clear ocean. You have never seen an ocean this crystal-clear before." The Lord held my hand and led the way. I shouted, "Lord, I am very frightened of the water. I do not think I can go in." As I resisted the Lord comforted me, held my hand, and led me into the water.

With comforting words, the Lord said, "Yoo-Kyung, do not worry about anything. Just hold on to My hands as we swim." Then the Lord and I began to swim. At first, I felt awkward and scared; however, as I continued to swim, it became fun. I was swimming. I was enjoying myself, splashing and swimming, when a lamb walked across the beach. Instantly, the Lord was on shore petting the lamb.

Jesus waved and said, "Yoo-Kyung, come here and pet the lamb." I swam to shore and approached the lamb. As I petted the lamb, I noticed how the fur was so soft and fluffy. It was very smooth. I picked up the lamb and embraced it, but I think it was uncomfortable with me since it began to cry as I held it. The Lord Jesus leaned over and said, "Yoo-Kyung, it is enough for today. Let us come back another time." I looked up and said, "Lord, I love You," and the Lord answered me, "Yes, I know." He escorted me back to the church on Earth.

DAY THIRTEEN

When Jesus came into the coasts of Caesarea Philippi, he asked his
disciples, saying, Whom do men say that I the Son of man am? And
they said, Some say that thou art John the Baptist: some, Elias; and
others, Jeremias, or one of the prophets. He saith unto them, But
whom say ye that I am? And Simon Peter answered and said, Thou
art the Christ, the Son of the living God. And Jesus answered and
said unto him, Blessed art thou, Simon Barjona: for flesh and blood
hath not revealed it unto thee, but my Father which is in heaven.
And I say also unto thee, That thou art Peter, and upon this rock I
will build my church; and the gates of hell shall not prevail against
it. And I will give unto thee the keys of the kingdom of heaven: and
whatsoever thou shalt bind on earth shall be bound in heaven: and
whatsoever thou shalt loose on earth shall be loosed in heaven.
—MATTHEW 16:13–19

Kim, Joo-Eun: Today during the sermon, the pastor requested the
congregation to concentrate our minds and thoughts as we prayed.
The pastor even made a remark to Meena, who was only five years old,
"Meena, when you pray today, do not open your eyes. Lift your hands
high and pray in tongues, as we will pray for a lengthy time." Meena
responded, "Amen."

The sermon seemed more passionate than any other day. Although
we were tired, the pastor tried to keep us awake by humoring us. Sister
Baek, Bong-Nyo witnessed the events just as I had.

AN ALL-OUT ATTACK
BY THE EVIL SPIRITS

During prayer time, the whole congregation was praying in tongues fervently. As we prayed, the evil spirit shaped as the crescent moon appeared to me again. Just as before, the evil spirit did not have a body but came in the form of a crescent moon. The crescent moon-shaped spirit had one eye shaped as a crescent moon and the other eye had its lids inverted and rolled back. Although it had no body, it walked around. At first this evil spirit had no mouth, but it was able to tear itself a mouth. With its newly formed mouth, it threatened me with its menacing shout. With confidence, I rebuked it several times in the name of Jesus, saying, "You filthy evil spirit. Depart." It disappeared.

While I was praying, I was transported to a dark place. Instantly, I knew it was hell. The place was dark. I could sense there was a large creature moving about. Within a short time, I began to vaguely see other creatures within my midst. I noticed many evil spirits. They were congregating around the large creature. The place was consumed with fire. The fire raged as flames rose all around. The area was very large, and I could see the accent of redness from the color of the flames. The large creature seemed to be agitated and fretful. It screamed and paced in all directions, as it appeared confused and restless.

The large creature became more vivid. It looked like a skeleton with long, white hair that came down to the shoulder. The large creature appeared to be the leader of the other evil spirits. The other evil spirits were countless in number. They were awaiting orders from the large creature, who would command their attack. After the command, the countless evil spirits flew into the air and appeared at our church. Their speed was instant; it felt like less than a second.

All the evil spirits attacked the congregation including Meena, the five year old. When Meena shouted sternly in tongues, "Babaya," an evil spirit next to her fell back. The attack was all at once, and it affected those us of who were praying in tongues. The evil spirits all fell one by one.

PASTOR KIM IS ON SPIRITUAL FIRE—THE
DEVIL DARES NOT COME AROUND HIM

The demon shouted a command, "Listen, all of you. Attack Pastor Kim. If the leadership falls, the rest will easily fall. You idiots, what are you waiting for? Attack Pastor Kim with full force," it said. Suddenly, a large amount of evil spirits from outside and inside the church appeared and attacked Pastor Kim. But what happened next was very surprising—many of the evil spirits that attacked fell where they stood. The evil spirits were injured and defeated. They were all frightened from what had happened so suddenly.

I was very surprised at what had happened, and I looked at the pastor in amazement. Once again, the evil force attempted to attack, but they were defeated in all directions. The attacks continued, but the result ended up the same. They could not touch the pastor.

Before this event, I thought the footsteps I heard were the pastor's, walking side to side on the altar. But I later found out that it was the sound of the evil spirits falling to the ground as they attempted to attack the pastor. When the evil spirits realized that their attacks were useless, they all became frightened and avoided him. They only hovered around him and would not dare to go closer to the pastor.

As I was praying in tongues, I looked at the pastor. He was not aware of what had happened. He was fervently praying in tongues on his knees and raising his hands high. I had so desired to receive the prayer of fire. As the evil spirits hovered around the pastor, he prayed in tongues with a thunderous voice. Then the frightened evil spirits flew toward the wall and broke into pieces. They all cried out in terror. When I saw the evil spirits fleeing, I felt triumphant and laughed victoriously.

Then I saw the devil shouting in anger, "Pastor Kim, do not pray. Do you think we will let you get away like this? I will kill you, I swear it." Then it gnashed its teeth. Then it shouted once again, this time at its demons, "You idiots. With all your strength you cannot even handle one pastor? Hurry and attack!"

Then the devil shouted, "Oh, that pastor is so much of a headache. Ahh, I think I am going insane. Just leave Pastor Kim alone and let us attack the congregation. Hurry." The force began to attack the congregation, but when they attacked the congregation, they did not attack them with full strength. They attacked with one to three evil spirits per person, not with full force.

THE CONGREGATION IS EQUIPPED WITH THE SHIELD OF PRAYER

The evil spirits spread out in all directions and this time decided to attack every person in the congregation. There were all kinds of evil spirits, and they all came in different forms and shapes. Because of the great number, it is impossible to describe all of them. However, no matter how fiercely they attacked, the evil spirits failed to succeed. The congregation's prayer in tongues provided the strength and power to repel the evil spirits. As they attacked, they also fell back. As the night continued, the prayers of the congregation became more intense and powerful.

The king of the evil spirits shouted, "People of The Lord's Church, stop praying. Why do you continue to pray? Evil spirits, what are you doing? Can't any one of you stop them?" The subordinate evil spirits ran about in pandemonium. It did not matter how many the king of evil spirits sent. The prayers by the brave congregation defeated them all.

The five-year-old Meena prayed for four hours that day, nonstop. I was also praying in tongues intensely. During my prayer, an evil spirit with a long, white dress appeared before me. The evil spirit had long, black hair with long sharp nails. It ran toward me and as it ran the evil spirit raised its hand in an attempt to thrust its long, sharp nails into me. I was very appalled and frightened by the sound and actions of the spirit. It moved hastily toward me, but it could not attack me. I was very frightened as it hovered around me. Then I screamed out loud.

Suddenly an evil spirit in the form of a skeleton approached me. The surface of the skull displayed numerous boils and blemishes, like a person with leprosy. The evil spirit lunged its skull at me. I became startled and shouted for Jesus, "Lord Jesus, please help me." But Jesus did not respond. I shouted once more with all my strength, "Filthy, despicable spirits. In the name of Jesus Christ, depart from me now." As I shouted, the evil spirits chattered their teeth stating, "Stop praying. I will distract and disturb you so that you cannot pray. I will curse you with sickness. Ha ha ha ha," they laughed wickedly.

I replied, "What? You despicable spirits." I felt nauseous. The spirit in the long, white dress and the skeleton with the grotesque skull were still harassing me. The spirit in the long, white dress moved about hastily in the air. The skeleton continued to lunge at me. I commanded once more, "In the name Jesus, depart from me now." Both of the evil spirits began to move toward Sister Yoo-Kyung. As they moved toward her, I could hear her prayers get louder.

The evil spirits turned toward Meena. I did not know if Meena could spiritually see the evil spirits or not. However, I noticed her prayer in tongues became more intense, and she shouted in tongues, "Babaya." The evil spirits disappeared.

I regained my focus and concentration and continued to pray. Without any rest, another evil spirit in the form of a beheaded person dangled close to the church ceiling. It looked right at me. I cast it out in the name of Jesus.

MANY COFFINS IN HELL
ARE FILLED WITH PASTORS

As I continued to pray in tongues, the sight of hell suddenly appeared before my eyes. I saw the devil jabbing a long, sharp weapon into rectangular shaped boxes. With foul language, it shouted, "You think you are a pastor? What kind of life did you live? I am ecstatic that you are here with me." The evil spirit continued to jab the rectangular boxes as it cursed. Loud, painful screams permeated from the boxes. I then saw blood gush and flow out from the boxes.

I cried for hours as I witnessed the sight. I called to the Lord many times, "Lord, where are You? I am so frightened." After some time, the Lord appeared next to me and held my hand. Jesus spoke to me, "Joo-Eun, observe the scene before you very carefully." I looked closely at the rectangular boxes. The tops of the boxes were covered with a canvass. A large cross was portrayed on the canvas. The boxes were lined up in an orderly fashion, and they stretched endlessly. I could not see where the number of boxes ended. There were small, round holes on each side of the box. I realized they were caskets. The evil spirits were jabbing their long, sharp spears into the holes unmercifully.

Curious, I asked the Lord, "Jesus, why are the caskets of former pastors here?" The Lord replied, "These pastors did not preach My gospel. They preached another gospel, and those who followed became depraved. This is their end result, a place in hell." I said, "Jesus, I remember reading the same torment from the book, *Revelations of Hell*. I am witnessing what I have read before." The Lord answered, "You are right. Depraved pastors will be judged greater."

ADULTERERS SUFFER IN THE FRYING PAN

We soon arrived at a different place in hell. Once we arrived, I became nauseous from the smell of grease and burning oil. It had an awful smell that churned my stomach. Soon after, a large frying pan appeared in front of me. It startled me and I turned away. However, I was able to get a glimpse as my curiosity got the best of me. I decided to look, and I noticed a sticky, thick, greasy substance. Within the sticky substance, I witnessed a numerous amount of people running around inside the frying pan. As they ran, they all screamed in pain, "Hot! Hot!"

The bottom of the frying pan glowed red from the fierce fire that raged below. The torment began as the people were placed side by side like sardines. As the heat increased, the people jumped up in pain and then ran in circles.

As oil touched their bodies, their flesh would disintegrate and only their bones would remain. They ran as skeletons, and the cycle continued as their flesh would return. Once they became whole, they would once again lay down side by side. Their torment became an endless cycle. I could hear their continuous groans, wailing, and loud, bitter weeping. All I heard was, "Hot. Ahh, help!"

I became frightened as they jumped chaotically. I began to cry. As I cried, the Lord covered my ears with His hands and said, "Joo-Eun, do not listen to the sounds of their cries." Crying, I said, "Lord, the odor of burning flesh is suffocating me. I feel like vomiting." Then Jesus touched my nose. After He touched my nose, I could no longer smell the odor of burning flesh.

I was compelled to ask the Lord what sin they had committed to suffer such torment. The Lord replied, "When they were in the world, they committed adultery against their spouses. They committed their acts in secret. And for their sin, they are in torment."

Jesus held my hand and led me to another place in hell. Soon after, we arrived at a pit. The pit was very large. It must have been deep since I could not see the bottom. The pit was filled with a multitude of people. The pit was consumed with fire, and the flames shot over the pit. The fire was so strong that I could feel the heat from a distance. I was apprehensive about getting too close. The red-hot fire appeared as though it had a life of its own. People were running inside the pit. They were screaming from the intense heat. The air was filled with the smell of burning flesh. The pit produced endless smoke from the fuel of human flesh. The smoke rose continuously.

Jesus explained about these people, "These are the people who believed in a false religion or those who rejected the gospel." The Lord took my hand and told me we should go. As soon as He finished speaking, I was already transported back to the church and praying in tongues.

YOO-KYUNG'S TRIP TO HEAVEN

Lee, Yoo-Kyung: While I was fervently praying in tongues, an evil spirit appeared before me in the form of a bat. It came toward me as it flapped its wings. The bat's shoulders did not have any flesh; I could only see the bones. On its face, I could only see two eyes and no other features. As it came near, I cast it out in the name of Jesus. Soon after, Jesus appeared and said, "Yoo-Kyung, let us go to heaven." He held my hand, and we quickly arrived in heaven.

I entered a room filled with books. As I looked around, I noticed a Bible and a book on gospel songs made out of gold. As I turned the pages, I came upon my favorite song, "Silent Night." I began to sing it. Many of the angels were in charge of the library.

The Lord said to me, "Yoo-Kyung, I am very thankful that you evangelized today. Therefore, I will show you your house in heaven. Follow me." With excitement and joy, I followed Him. Suddenly, I saw a glittering treasure house and a tall house as high as a skyscraper.

Later, I told the Lord, "Lord, I want to visit and get a glimpse of hell." Jesus said, "Yoo-Kyung, heaven is filled with happiness and joy. But hell is the opposite. It is a horrible place filled with fear and death. If you are frequently exposed to hell, it will affect you in a negative way, and you may not observe it carefully. When the proper time comes, I will show you hell again. Therefore, do not worry."

ANGELS DEFEND QUICKLY

Lee, Haak-Sung: While I was praying in tongues with my eyes closed, a light flashed before me. With my awakened spiritual eyes, I saw a group of evil spirits running toward all the members in the congregation, and they began to attack each one of them.

Suddenly, one of the evil spirits appeared in the form of a man. That particular evil spirit had a hole on its left cheekbone. From its left hand, numerous cockroaches marched out from the ends of its fingers. The cockroaches began to crawl up the body of the evil spirit and they all climbed into the hole of the left cheekbone. As they crawled into the hole of the cheekbone, they negotiated inside the face and down the mouth. With a sardonic grin, the evil spirit chewed the cockroaches. The site was horrific. I then commanded the evil spirit to depart in Jesus's name. With my command, it disappeared. Another evil spirit in human form began to walk toward me. The evil spirit was covered with ticks, from its face to the rest of its body. It was another horrid-looking creature, and it walked close enough to touch my nose. I drove it out in Jesus's name. Another evil spirit appeared, this one with four faces. It had a face on the front and the back of its head, and on the sides of the face, where the ears usually are located. This spirit was very frightening and horrid looking. All four faces had a different appearance. It began to spin its head very rapidly. The evil spirit also had four hands and four feet. This was a unique-looking creature. Its bruised, curled tendons dangled from the joints and skin. The site was appalling, and I became frightened. I commanded it to leave in the name of Jesus. However, it did not comply, and startled me as it walked side to side. I prayed, "Jesus, I am scared. Please come now." But the Lord did not come. Apprehensively, I prayed in tongues more intensely. Then Jesus appeared. As soon as Jesus arrived, the evil spirit became startled and fled.

It was a very cold evening. Around 6:30 p.m., Joseph, Joo-Eun, Yoo-Kyung, and I got together at the pastor's home to pray before going out to evangelize. We were prepared, as we had materials to hand out. The Lord Jesus held Yoo-Kyung's hand as we went out evangelizing. The Lord, accompanied by His angels, had escorted us and followed every footstep. The Lord shielded us from the elements of the weather and kept us warm. During our evangelizing, Joseph had a difficult time walking. He was in great pain. However, the pain did not stop him from continuing the Lord's work. When we had finished evangelizing, we decided to go to church and pray.

Once we entered the church, I immediately noticed a group of evil spirits hovering above the altar close to the ceiling. We walked to the back of the church, turned off the lights, and began to pray with our hands lifted up. As we began to pray, the evil spirits started to scream and belligerently run toward us. As soon as the evil spirit shouted, all the evil spirits, including the ones that were hidden, appeared and charged toward us. Then Jesus suddenly appeared and quickly commanded the angels, "Angels, defend them quickly." Once the command was given, the angels that escorted the four youngsters during evangelism and five other angels from heaven quickly held hands to form a line of protection. The angels stood in front of us and protected us from the evil spirits. The charge from the evil spirits was halted.

The Lord commanded me to remove the socks from Joseph's feet. Once I removed the socks, the Lord applied His blood to the area where the pain was originating. The Lord said, "From this moment, you will not feel any more pain during your walks. It will heal gradually, and you will feel an itching sensation. Do not scratch your feet. If you scratch it, the problem will come back. Therefore, endure the itch."

MRS. KANG, HYUN-JA'S PATERNAL AND MATERNAL GRANDFATHERS IN HELL

Baek, Bong-Nyo: While I was in prayer, Jesus came and took me to a dark place in hell. Suddenly, the Lord and I were walking on a very narrow path. At the end of the narrow path we came to a large, open field. We gazed out over the large field. Although it was very dark, I somehow was able to view the surroundings. I observed two elderly gentlemen standing in the field. They stood motionless. They appeared in a state of misery. Their countenance made me feel sick to my stomach. As I continued to stare at them, I began to shake in fear. As I shook, the Lord tightly held my hand and said, "I will always be by your side. Do not be frightened."

"If the Lord ever takes you to hell for a visitation, please find out if my paternal and maternal grandfathers are there," requested Mrs. Kang, Hyun-Ja. The Lord already knew what I was reminiscing; therefore, He took me to the place where the grandfathers were tormented. The Lord showed me the place of torment for the two grandfathers. Snakes longer and bigger than anacondas squeezed them tightly. The snakes had coiled up to the grandfathers' heads. I could not comprehend the sight. The snakes were continuously coiling themselves into the mouths of the two grandfathers. Somehow, they were able to scream and shout, "Help!" As they shouted, the snakes coiled tighter, and it appeared the grandfathers were suffocating.

I stated to the Lord, "Jesus, Mrs. Kang, Hyun-Ja should be deeply praying by now. Can You please let her see for herself by opening her spiritual eyes? I hope she can have an opportunity to witness what I am seeing." The Lord did not reply; therefore, I persistently repeated the request. Then the Lord replied, "I will bring her here now, but she will not realize that she is in hell. I will not open her spiritual eyes. I will just bring her soul to this place. This way, her physical body will be able to feel the darkness." The Lord then brought her to the place where her grandfathers were being tormented.

As Jesus and I stood together, the soul of Mrs. Kang, Hyun-Ja stood in front of her grandfathers. The Lord spoke to the grandfathers, "This is your granddaughter who stands in front of you. Look closely. She is the one who lived with you." Once the Lord finished speaking, the two grandfathers started to shout as the snakes tightened their grip.

The two grandfathers began to talk, but it was as if they shouted, "Where? It is really our granddaughter? What a surprise. What are you doing here? Why did you come to this horrible place? If you witness me in torment, you will also feel pain. What is the purpose of your visit?" Mrs. Kang, Hyun-Ja became sad and began to wail. Although there were no tears, her prayer was a prayer of mourning.

As I watched the whole incident, tears ran down my face. The Lord said, "Bong-Nyo, you are physically weak and tired, do not cry. We will leave her here with them for a while. I want to show you a special past event. Let us go now." We went to heaven. Jesus showed me an event when some of the angels of God's kingdom became corrupt. The events I was shown were as clear as day.

After I had witnessed how some angels fell, the Lord and I returned to the place where Mrs. Kang, Hyun-Ja was standing. As we flew back, the Lord stated, "Perhaps Sister Hyun-Ja is still crying. Let us hurry." As soon as we arrived, Mrs. Kang, Hyun-Ja's soul was still standing and she was still sobbing as she prayed in tongues. The Lord compassionately looked at her and took pity.

The two grandfathers were still shouting. Every time they opened their mouths to talk, I could also see the head of a snake as it hissed with its tongue repeatedly. I could not comprehend how the grandfathers were able to speak as the snake coiled into their mouths. Nevertheless, I was able to hear them talk and shout very clearly. The maternal grandfather shouted, "Is it really you, granddaughter? Where are you? I want to see you, but I cannot see you because the snake is coiling around my head. I miss you very much. Where are you standing? Can you ask the Lord to uncoil the snake? Please, please ask Him to remove the snake. Once the snake is removed, you will not be able to see me, but I will be able to see you. I want to free my mouth so I can speak more clearly, and the snake is hindering me. Hyun-Ja, my dear granddaughter, I miss you very much." The grandfather was wailing and sobbing.

As I witness the sight, the sad events made me cry. Although I knew my request would be unlikely to be fulfilled, I asked the Lord anyway, "Please, Lord, let Mrs. Kang, Hyun-Ja see her grandfathers." The Lord did not reply. I continued to pray, "Lord, why are the grandfathers in this place?" The Lord explained, "While they were alive in the world, they were alcoholics and abused their wives. However, most importantly, they did not believe in Me. This is why they are here, and it is too late."

The paternal grandfather shouted and said, "My dear granddaughter, I wish to hold you in my arms one more time. I am tormented in hell. When I was in the world, I did not know the consequences. You probably do not know how I treated you grandmother. I abused her and broke her heart many times. You were very young at that time. I am very sorry. I regret everything. Please believe in the Lord with all your strength and heart. Pray earnestly. I want you to go to heaven and have eternal life. Do not ever come here. I wish to hold your hand, and I wish to hold you in my arms. However, the snake is hindering me. It is impossible." The two grandfathers began to cry hysterically.

Suddenly, the snakes began to coil the grandfathers with a stronger grip, and I could hear their bodies becoming broken. The grandfathers began to scream as their flesh exploded and ripped from their bones. Their bones shattered into pieces as well. It did not matter how much the grandfathers begged. It was futile. The Lord replied, "Your granddaughter married a pastor after she accepted Me as her Lord and Savior. She is now serving Me in the world."

Jesus said to me, "It is enough. Now let us go." However, before we even noticed, the bodies of the two grandfathers turned back to normal. Their bones, flesh, and skin all appeared normal. But of course, the snakes were still there coiling their bodies very tightly as their torment began again. The grandfathers all shouted and cried pitifully in pain. I tried to console them with some comforting words, but I knew it would be in vain. "Grandfathers, do not cry. I also have family members tormented by flames. Their pain is unbearable—my mother, father, and brother. I think your torment is less painful than the burning flames. My heart aches for you both."

The Lord said, "Let us go. We do not have much time." He grabbed Mrs. Kang, Hyun-Ja's hand and then my hand and led us back to our church. When we arrived at the church, I saw the physical body of Mrs. Kang, Hyun-Ja in motion as she prayed. She was shaking her head side-to-side and praying in tongues. She was not praying with her usual body posture. I could see the expression on her face. It was an expression of sorrow. Her lamentable prayers pierced my heart as I felt her pain.

The next day my whole body severely ached. I had to pray while lying down in bed. The Holy Spirit gave me the strength to pray. As I prayed, I received a vision from the Lord. He gave me a vision of hell and commanded me to record the details. Whenever I visit hell, my whole body aches in pain. It takes me a few days to recover.

THE SECOND SERVICE PRAYER MEETING:
PRAISE HIM, OH MY SOUL

And they shall mock him, and shall scourge him, and shall spit upon him, and shall kill him: and the third day he shall rise again. And James and John, the sons of Zebedee, come unto him, saying, Master, we would that thou shouldest do for us whatsoever we shall desire. And he said unto them, What would ye that I should do for you? They said unto him, Grant unto us that we may sit, one on thy right hand, and the other on thy left hand, in thy glory. But Jesus said unto them, Ye know not what ye ask: can ye drink of the cup that I drink of? and be baptized with the baptism that I am baptized with?

—MARK 10:34–38

Lee, Yoo-Kyung: After early morning services we began to pray. While I was fervently praying and calling out to Jesus, He came and held my hand. "Yoo-Kyung, would you like to praise and sing a song while holding My hand?" I replied, "Yes." I sang and praised with the Lord. The song we sang was "Praise Him, Oh My Soul." We sang it over and over. Jesus went to Mrs. Kang, Hyun-Ja and comforted her while she was praying. She was earnestly praying in tears. The Lord sat next to her and spoke consoling words. The Lord returned to me and said, "Yoo-Kyung, be obedient to Mrs. Kang, Hyun-Ja." The Lord then returned to Mrs. Kang, Hyun-Ja.

BALD HEAD SUITS PASTOR KIM

Kim, Joo-Eun: While the pastor prayed at the altar, the Lord Jesus came and stood next to the pastor. The Lord patted the pastor's bald head, and while laughing, He said, "Ha ha ha ha ha, bald head Pastor Kim." As I saw the Lord with the pastor, I clamorously laughed as I was praying. Before the prayer meeting, the pastor had wished that Jesus would come and compliment him about his bald head. Later, the Lord said, "Pastor Kim, you really do pray fervently. In fact, you look good bald-headed. I don't know if I should help you with you losing your hair," and He laughed out loud.

Despite of the cold weather, we continued to pray until early morning. After my conversation with the Lord, I continued to pray fervently. As I prayed, a crescent moon-shaped evil spirit walked toward me. Its eyes were uneven in size and shape, but I boldly cast it out in the name of Jesus. Soon after, an evil spirit disguised as a young girl with a white dress appeared. It looked very frightening. It had long, dark hair, which went down to its waist. There was blood dribbling around her mouth. It had sharp fangs like Dracula's. It tried to frighten me. Another evil spirit appeared and made a horrible sound; however, I cast them all out in the name of Jesus.

After our prayer meeting, we all ate rice balls. It was very delicious. As usual, as we went home from praying, the sunrise greeted us.

DAY FOURTEEN

I marvel that ye are so soon removed from him that called
you into the grace of Christ unto another gospel: Which is
not another; but there be some that trouble you, and would
pervert the gospel of Christ. But though we, or an angel from
heaven, preach any other gospel unto you than that which we
have preached unto you, let him be accursed. As we said before,
so say I now again, If any man preach any other gospel unto
you than that ye have received, let him be accursed. For do I
now persuade men, or God? or do I seek to please men? for
if I yet pleased men, I should not be the servant of Christ.

—GALATIANS 1:6–10

EVIL SPIRITS CONTINUALLY APPEARING

Kim, Joo-Eun: I was fervently praying when a unique looking evil
spirit appeared. It was a grotesque skeleton with long, white hair and
a lanky face. I began to pray in tongues through my heart and not
verbally as I waited for the evil spirit to draw closer. When it drew
closer, I shouted, "In the name of Jesus, depart." It then disappeared
immediately. Once the evil spirit departed, I felt confident and victorious with my faith.

After a little while, an evil spirit disguised as a young woman with
a white dress appeared. When it drew toward me, I noticed blood
dribbling from its mouth. The evil spirit said, "Do not pray. I am
going to defeat you." It then motioned and prepared to attack me, but
I replied, "You filthy evil spirit, in the name of Jesus, depart from me."
It departed. Then another evil spirit appeared. This time it looked like

a red dragon. It was very angry, and it slowly walked toward me. The dragon did not have a body, only a head and face. I felt like it could swallow me whole. It glanced at me in a very menacing way as it turned its head. I was very frightened by the evilness in its eyes.

Many more evil spirits began to appear. As I prayed more fervently, I sensed stronger evil spirits manifesting. I felt my spirit approaching closer to heaven. The evil spirits were attempting to block me from entering heaven by frightening me. Therefore, I zealously prayed in tongues with my eyes closed. I then continued to cast them out, "All of you filthy evil spirits, in the name of Jesus, depart from me." However, the red-faced dragon resisted. I commanded it in a louder voice, "In the name of Jesus, you filthy Satan, depart. Depart!" It still resisted. I continued and did not lose heart. As I persisted with the commands in Jesus's name, the evil spirit finally departed.

The Lord came, and He looked very impressed with me, a youngster like myself casting out evil spirits. Jesus called me by my nickname and my real name, "Joo-Eun, Freckles, your faith has increased dramatically, so continue to pray zealously with your eyes closed."

I concentrated as I prayed, and suddenly I felt darkness overwhelm me, with a cool breeze blowing against me. I saw a door open from a distance. Suddenly, a bright light appeared. I almost opened my eyes as the piercing light became strong, but I realized I was not able to open my eyes. Fear began to overwhelm me and then Jesus appeared. He began to explain, "Joo-Eun, while you were praying in tongues, your spirit was drawing near heaven with the escort of angels. However, the evil spirits appeared to frighten you so that you would open your eyes. But I intervened and commanded the evil spirits to depart. It was I who prevented you from opening your eyes. Joo-Eun, I think you need to pray a little more. I do not think you will go to heaven today." I thought to myself, "It was the filthy evil spirits that prevented me from going to heaven." I was greatly disappointed. Jesus then comforted me with encouraging words, "Joo-Eun, do not worry. I promise you that I will take you to heaven and show you around."

I asked the Lord a silly question, "Jesus, when the pastor preaches during service, he often calls Brother Haak-Sung, Brother Joseph, Sister Yoo-Kyung, and I by our nicknames. However, the pastor never calls the adults by their nicknames. Can You give them nicknames? By the way, the pastor calls his wife 'Bong Ja Ya, Bon Ja Sa Mo,' to tease her. But I think the pastor's wife does not like to be called by such nicknames."

Jesus replied, "Bong-Ja? Hmm...if she does not like to be called by that nickname, since her real name is Hyun-Ja, how about Sa-Bong or Sa-Mo? Provide her with those two options." Lastly, I asked the Lord, "Lord, will You bless us financially?" Jesus replied, "Financial blessing will come if you pray zealously and earnestly." And with that, our prayer meeting ended.

Lee, Haak-Sung: After some time in prayer, an evil spirit like a two-headed snake appeared. I screamed with a loud voice since it startled and frightened me. Although I was praying in tongues with authority and confidence, the evil spirit would not disappear or depart. In fact, it began to draw closer to me. This two-headed snake spirit was larger than any anaconda I could imagine or had seen in the movies. The heads of the snake resembled king cobras with their long tongues. The demon hissed at me. I became more frightened as the snake hissed in front of my face.

I cried very much during my prayer and shouted to the Lord for help as the two-headed snake harassed me. "Jesus, Lord, please come quickly. Where are You? Help me." No matter how many times I called for Jesus, the Lord did not appear. It seemed as though the evil spirit had waited for this moment, as it began to coil slowly around my legs and up to my stomach, chest, and then my neck. When it had coiled up to my neck, it began to tighten its grip. I could not breathe, and the evil spirit continued to suffocate me. Although I was losing my ability to breathe, I was still able to call upon the Lord. I called the Lord again and again. Then, suddenly the snake opened its mouth as wide as possible, gesturing to swallow me. With its mouth wide open, it began to hunch over to swallow me headfirst. As I nervously watched, the Lord suddenly appeared and grabbed the snake. He threw the snake away from me. The Lord asked, "Haak-Sung, are you afraid? Do not be afraid. I will protect you."

Those Within the Boiling Pot Cry Out in Agony

Jesus said, "I will show you hell. Observe it closely." The Lord held my hand, and in an instant we were in a dark place. Very clearly I could see the dark red flames burning around us. As we continued to walk, a large pot came before our sight. My jaw dropped as I witnessed the enormous size of the pot. I was totally stunned. As I was shown what was inside, I was appalled and startled.

There was dark black water boiling inside the huge pot. The intense red flames covered the exterior of the pot as it heated the water. The water was beyond the boiling point, as the bubbles created by the heated rose to the top. The steam created by the heat looked like smoke. As I was shown the inside of the pot, I saw multitudes of people inside the pot. There were men and women all crying out for help.

The cried out constantly, "Ahh! It is very hot. I cannot bear it anymore. I am in agony. Please help me. Please stop this torment." All of their flesh had deteriorated from the boiling water. Their bones were floating and bouncing in the hot water. Although they had lost their flesh and form, the bones were crying out in agony and somehow they were able to continue feeling pain. I could smell the awful odor of burning, boiling flesh and bones. I wanted to vomit, as the stench made it difficult to breathe. As the pot began to boil fiercely, the dark smoke filled the air and made it difficult to see. If I had not been there with Jesus, I would have fainted from the sight and odor. The Lord held my hand and said, "Let us go a little farther." With my trust in the Lord, we moved to another place in hell.

THE PLACE OF TORMENT FOR FORTUNE-TELLERS AND SUICIDE VICTIMS

As we walked farther inside, there was a large evil creature sitting on a chair. Its posture and demeanor suggested it was a king in this domain. A large trapdoor was located on the floor in front of the feet of the creature. People were standing on top of the trapdoor. A white line was visible between the creature's feet and the trapdoor. When the creature stomped on the white line, the door opened downward, dropping the people. As I was able to glance into the opened trapdoor, I realized below was volcanic lava. As the people fell into the boiling lava, they instantly caught fire and screamed in pain.

I was very frightened by what I saw. I asked the Lord, "Jesus, who are these people? Why are they tormented in lava? I feel so sorry for them. I do not want to witness this anymore. They are helplessly seeking hope." Jesus replied, "These people were fortune-tellers, the customers of fortune-tellers, sorcerers, witches, and people who committed suicide."

When the Lord spoke of suicide victims, my uncle, who committed suicide by overdosing on pills, came into my sight. When my uncle and I made eye contact with one another, I screamed, "Uncle, it's me, Haak-Sung. Why are you standing on the trapdoor?" My uncle was next in line to stand over the trapdoor. The next group with my uncle was dragged to the trapdoor and made to stand. The creature lifted its leg up to stomp on the line and release the doors.

I begged the Lord for mercy, "Please, Jesus, my uncle is in danger of falling into the lava. Please help him." In more agony, I cried out louder, "Lord, my uncle was always nice to me. Uncle, come to my side quickly." With a sad expression, the Lord said, "Haak-Sung, it is too late. There is nothing that can be done." My uncle looked at me and said, "Haak-Sung, please hold my hand." The moment my uncle stretched his hand forward, the creature stomped his foot, and the trapdoors opened. The group fell down into the lava as the people screamed.

Among the people in this domain of torment—those who did not

113

know God—many were Buddhist monks, some were backslidden Christians, and there were some who attended church for reasons other than for Jesus. There were many diverse and different kinds of helpless people who were led onto the trapdoor and down into the lava. Jesus meticulously explained what I was witnessing. I could not stop crying. I was very frightened. As I cried, the Lord encouraged me to walk with Him a little farther.

As we walked a little farther, a large object appeared. It looked like a waterwheel, but it could have been a large tire. Nevertheless, it was large and round. The large round object rotated continuously. The object was covered with sharp, pointed blades. A dark, red glow resonated from the tip of each blade, and I could sense and feel the heat from them.

As the large circular object rotated, I saw men and women lying beneath the object. They were all crowded together like sardines. The object rotated, pressing the blade into the victims without mercy.

I could not watch anymore. It was a horrific sight. The sharp blades pierced and ripped into the victims' bodies. The peoples' bodies would explode like water balloons. Once the circular object finished its job, a group of evil creatures began to clean up the body parts. They cleaned without any respect. They treated the body parts as garbage. After they had gathered all the body parts, the evil creatures would throw them into the volcano. It was a gruesome sight.

This place in hell was full of volcanoes. All the volcanoes appeared ready to erupt. It was also a place that housed many creatures that wore black bracelets. Each creature carried a large club made of iron. They used the club mercilessly on people who resisted and those who tried to escape the volcano.

These were creatures I had already encountered while praying in tongues at the church. These were the evil spirits or creatures that attempted to approach me. The multitude of creatures all looked similar to one another. The creatures enjoyed tormenting and scorching the people.

FICKLE INDIVIDUALS

Jesus said, "Haak-Sung, watch closely." There were many people surrounded by large and small snakes. They were all mingled tightly together. The large snakes coiled around the heads of the people while the small snakes coiled around the peoples' bodies. The small snakes would continuously strike and bite. The people hollered out in pain.

I asked the Lord, "Lord, what kind of sin did these people commit?" The Lord replied, "They never had true faith in Me. They never believed in Me with a true heart. Even when they claimed to believe in Me, their works were not consistent. They were capricious. Their capricious behavior affected their church attendance. They were never truly born again. Most of them all died in accidents, and they were not able to repent completely. Haak-Sung, even you have a capricious personality. However, your Christian walk is stable," the Lord told me.

There were many pits filled with fire. The fire looked like it had a life of its own. The flames would burst very high. Jesus grabbed my hand and said that we should continue. We walked for a good distance and arrived at a very large place. There were several large walls. They were so large I could not see their end. The walls were rotating in a clockwise direction, while some were rotating in a counter-clockwise direction. There were some that would flip over continuously in one direction and others in other directions.

On the surface of the walls, there were multitudes of men and women lying against the wall with their hands and legs tied together. The people were tied next to one another with no space in between each other.

In a short time, I heard a hissing noise come from all directions. Then, suddenly, a fire containing different colors appeared. The fire glowed with red, yellow, and blue colors. The fire began to burn the flesh and clothes off the people. The people screamed and shouted for help. As the walls rotated, the people were literally roasted until all the flesh was burned from their bones. Once they were complete skeletons, I saw the wall rotate, and when the people reappeared, they had regained their flesh. Large snakes appeared and began to coil around their heads.

Horrific green creatures with long, slender eyes appeared. The shape and look of the eyes reminded me of a fox, for foxes have such eyes. The creature had a triangular-shaped nose with a horn on each side of its head. It had three fingers on its hand. The creature was so obese that it almost looked as if its body were swollen. Each creature carried a club with sharp thorns. They rushed the people from all directions and mercilessly assaulted them. The people all cried out hopelessly for help.

As the people cried out, "Help, please!" the creatures struck at the peoples' heads. And when they shouted, "Please untie us!" the creatures bashed the peoples' bodies with clubs. I noticed a woman crying out very loudly, "This is unfair! I do not deserve this type of punishment. My life on Earth was miserable. I could not bear it anymore. That is why I committed suicide. However, the pain in hell is more unbearable than life on Earth. Why did you send me to hell? It is not fair. I had never heard about the realities of hell. It is unfair for me to be here." She repeated it over and over.

One of the evil creatures laughed and replied, "I completely deceived you into committing suicide. You did not know the truth. You even attended church but never heard about heaven or hell. I was even apprehensive of your learning of this place. Although you attended church, you still killed yourself. Therefore, it is fair for you to be here. I outsmarted and deceived you. I won your soul. I will show many lessons for all eternity." The creature began to bash and beat the woman mercilessly.

I cried as I watched the horrendous sight. I was so frightened. Jesus stood closer and comforted me. He wiped my tears and held me tight in His arms. The torment and pain would be endless and eternal. The screams and pleas for mercy would go unanswered. It is eternal torment. The Lord and I left and came out of hell.

When I arrived at church, I began to pray in tongues. The Lord said to me, "Haak-Sung, your prayers that last from night until early in the morning are much more competent and powerful than your prayers during the day. Therefore, try to pray more at night rather than during the day." He told me to look closer at Him. I saw the Lord wearing a crown of thorns on His head, and I saw the holes in His hands and His feet. There was blood flowing from each wound. I kept repenting and cried out as I watched the Lord's suffering.

Then I finished praying. After praying, the Lord took me to heaven and wiped away my tears. When I arrived in heaven, I was at heaven's ocean, which was crystal clear.

CAN I STAY IN HEAVEN?

Lee, Yoo-Kyung: As I was praying fervently, Jesus came and spoke to me, "Did you miss Me?" I happily replied, "Yes, very much, Lord." The Lord said, "How much did you miss Me?" I raised my hands over my head and drew a heart with my arms and fingers. With a loud voice I said, "Jesus, I love You."

I felt great that day. Usually evil spirits harass me when I start my prayers. But that day, the Lord met me. He not only appeared, but He took me to heaven. Jesus said, "You feel good today, don't you?" I replied, "Yes, Lord. I feel great because I did not see evil spirits today." After we arrived in heaven, one of the angels leaned over and said to me, "Wow. You here again? You must feel great to come here so often." Then the angel smiled at me.

The Lord took me to a very high place and showed me the Earth. The Earth appeared very small from such a high distance. I observed the Earth spinning. Jesus pointed at the Earth and said, "There is your country, where your city and home are located." I asked the Lord, "Jesus, I want to live in heaven. I do not want to go back to the Eearth." Jesus replied, "It is not your time now. You first have to serve Me and zealously do My work. At an appointed time, you will come here."

The Lord and I spent quality time in heaven. We made jokes and laughed a lot. We had a good time. I enjoyed it very much. The Lord and I returned to church.

HIGH-VOLTAGE IRON BARS IN HELL

Baek, Bong-Nyo: As we were praying, Jesus appeared among us. He suddenly stopped walking and began to murmur to Himself, "Who should I choose to visit hell?" I found out later that He was murmuring in front of me because He had already decided to take me to visit hell. When He stood in front of me, I was apprehensive. He said to me, "I have many things to show you. Let us go together."

The Lord took my hand. Within that moment, I reminisced about my conversation with the pastor. The pastor said, "My father and my oldest sister are probably in hell because they had not accepted Christ. If the Lord takes me to hell and I can see with my own eyes, then I can write confidently the details of hell. I do not understand why the Lord will not let me visit hell." The pastor asked me to ask the Lord if He would show me the pastor's father and oldest sister if I were given the opportunity to visit hell.

On our way to visit hell, I therefore asked the Lord of the pastor's request. The Lord agreed to show me where the pastor's father and sister were. The Lord held my hand with a tight grip. He reminded me not to be afraid. He stated that I would see some frightening scenes and that He would protect me. As He finished speaking to me, we were walking along a narrow pathway. The pathway was very dark. I could not see a thing. I lost all sense of direction. I could not comprehend if I was walking straight, backwards, or sideways. I could only be lead by Jesus. The Lord Himself was a light, and He shined through the darkness.

While we walked through, I began to hear very loud noises from all directions. The noise pierced my head and my ears began to hurt from the noise. I felt as though my head were going to explode. I began to recognize the noises; they became more vivid and clear. There were cries and shouting. It sounded like a demonstration or riot. I heard foul language against God. People were cursing one another, and it sounded like they were fighting. It was the sounds of chaos. The words I heard and the loudness hurt my ears and my soul.

The narrow path was endlessly long, and it felt like we were walking forever. Suddenly, I felt a presence passing very quickly around me. The Lord said, "Observe closely." He waved His hand, and I was able to see all. On each side of the narrow pathway there were large, wide chambers. The chambers were so large I could not see the end of the ceiling. The chambers were lined next to one another. Each chamber housed multitudes of people packed and cramped together. They had no room to move. The chambers were as tall as skyscrapers in major cities. There were iron bars in front of the chambers; it reminded me of jail cells. High voltage electricity ran through the iron bars. It reminded me of mosquito zappers, the ones that kill the bugs as they fly into the glowing light.

People were fighting and pushing one another in a futile attempt to avoid the iron bars. People were pushed against the electrical iron bars. The electricity zapped their flesh and caught fire. The victims burned, and only ashes would remain. Suddenly I heard a cry within the crowd. The man shouted and pleaded to us to help: "Lord, when I was on Earth, I went to church for food. However, I snuck out to drink and smoke during the sermons. But I died in a car accident and found myself in hell. Lord, please, I beg You to take me out of this place. Please, Lord. I will never do such sins again."

He began to cry louder as the Lord returned no answer. However, I noticed a strange event. When the man finished pleading to the Lord, his flesh began to disintegrate, and he became a skeleton. But he was still able to speak, "Lord, please take me out of this place. If you rescue me, I will never drink or smoke. I will never take advantage of the food from the church. I'll dedicate my life to prayer. If You command me to fast, I will fast as long as You wish it. I will fast a thousand years, or even ten thousand years. I'll dedicate my life to You and prayer. Please just take me out of this horrible place. Please!" As the man pleaded, his body came in contact with the high voltage. The moment his bones touched, he caught on fire and turned into ashes.

I heard another person next to the man pleading. The voice was feeble; it was a woman's voice. However, the voice became louder and sharper, "Lord, I do not deserve to be here. This is unfair. I did not know such place existed. Please, Lord, take me out of here." The Lord replied to her, "I meticulously know every single sin you have committed. How dare you lie to Me," He rebuked her. She then suddenly changed her tone. She became aggressive and spoke belligerent words, "Lord, what good deed have You done? If You are the true God and have the ability to save us, why did we end up here? Couldn't You have saved us? It is Your fault that multitudes are in hell." She was very disrespectful to the Lord.

The Lord was silent as the woman insulted Him. She was very arrogant. The rude woman continued to curse the Lord, "Hey, You, what have You done for us?" She would then turn and plead gently. Her attitude would change back and forth from pleading to arrogance. It was difficult for me to hear the woman insult the Lord. But the Lord stood in silence and gave her an audience.

The woman again began to shout and yell at the Lord. She pointed her finger and began to curse and use foul language. "You really think you are Lord of all? Look, even this very moment there are multitudes of people in hell. When I see a few hundred enter heaven, there are several hundred thousand entering hell. Look at these chambers. They are too many people in here. It is too crowded!"

When the multitudes realized it was the Lord, they all tried to converse with Him. They all reached out to Him with their hands. However, as they tried to reach out to Him, they were all zapped by the electrical iron bars and burnt to ashes. Although they were zapped and burnt to ashes, they all still attempted to rush close to the Lord. The people in the back who could not reach the Lord began to curse Him.

As the people shouted, the Lord stood in silence. He listened as they cursed and shouted. I begged the Lord, "Lord, let us please go. I have a bad headache. I am having a hard time breathing. I cannot bear it anymore." The Lord answered, "Very well." He tightly held my hand and told me that we needed to go a little farther.

My Mother in Torment
at Each Location in Hell

After we walked farther in, I witnessed another horrible sight. I arrived at the place of my mother's torment. She was in agony and in terrible pain. I never desired to witness my mother's torment again. I said to the Lord, "It is my mother. What should I do?" My mother was tormented at different places in hell. I was given the opportunity to witness her torment from beginning to present. Whenever the Lord and I arrived at a place in hell, my mother was there to be tormented. My mother was screaming in pain from the fire and heat. I could not bear it. I was in shock and fell. However, the Lord assisted me in getting back up. I continued to watch the awful scene.

"Mother! My poor mother, are you still here?" As I was shouting, my mother heard me and responded by crying. Crying hysterically, my mother yelled in pain, "Ouch! It is so hot. Bong-Nyo, I would rather be tormented some other way. I am tormented in unbearable heat. I am tormented with either hot water or fire. I hate it so much. Ouch! It is too hot. Bong-Nyo, take me out of here." As I watched, my mother's flesh disintegrated, and nothing but her bones was left. Even though I knew my question would not be possible, I decided to ask the Lord anyway. I could not bear to see my mother in terrible torment. It was too much for me. "Lord, please help her. Please." I began sob as I begged the Lord. No matter how much I cried, I knew my request was impossible. The Lord said, "It is too late. It is impossible to help her." The Lord grabbed my hand and began to drag me as I resisted. As the Lord dragged me, I kept looking back at my mother.

I continued, "Mother! My dear mother, what am I supposed to do? Mother, what am I supposed to do?" As I shouted in anguish, my mother replied as she cried, "Bong-Nyo, my daughter." My mother called my name over and over. Within minutes, I was only able to hear the faint echoes of her call.

Once we had left that place, the Lord and I arrived at another tormenting place. Once again, I witnessed my mother in torment. It

121

was only a short distance from where I had seen my mother, but she was now at that place. I noticed a large, evil creature. It appeared to be some king or prince of that place. As soon as the creature realized I was looking at my mother, the creature coiled its tongue around her. The creature's tongue reminded me of a snake.

My mother appeared as though she was suffocating, but she was still able to shout, "Bong-Nyo, why have you come again? If you are not able to save or rescue me, why have you come again? Why keep coming? Don't just stand there and watch, come rescue me. Please. Do you wish to see me in torment? Hurry and go. Do not ever come back again." When she finished yelling at me, the evil creature threw her into the burning flames. Once her body touched the flames, she burned instantaneously. I heard her awful screams.

TORMENTED GAMBLERS

The Lord commanded me to move forward. I was covered in tears and sweat. I did not want to go forward. I had seen enough. But I knew the Lord wanted me to see more. Another horrible scene was awaiting me. I saw multitudes of people sitting in a row. I noticed their arms and legs were stretched forward. A large creature with an enormous axe was pacing in front of the multitude. The axe appeared sharp and menacing.

The creature hacked the arms and legs off meticulously. He would start at the fingers and work his way up the arm up to the shoulder. The creature did the same with the legs. He first hacked the toes off and then moved up the legs. It was merciless and fast. The people screamed in pain. There was no end.

The people waiting to be chopped had the face of death. Their faces were frozen like ice. The creature sang and hummed as it hacked and chopped the people. The creature would use its enormous axe to easily hack the bones in half. Even the thicker bones were easily crushed. It looked like a person chopping wood. The flesh from the thinner bones quickly sliced away.

I was so frightened. As I was crying, I asked the Lord, "Lord, I am so scared. Why are these people here?" The Lord replied, "These are professional gamblers. The deceived many people in many ways. They never listened to anyone. Even if their hands, feet, or head were cut off, they would not have listened to anyone or repented. Their destiny was hell."

Once their hands and feet were cut off, the bodies would roll away. But soon after, their body parts would reattach, and the process of hacking would continue again. The people looked like dolls as they sat with no hands and feet. They were all crying in pain.

I noticed a familiar face among the crowd. I drew closer to get a clear look. I was shocked. It was my father. Our eyes locked on one another. My father was next in line to be chopped. I have unpleasant memories of my father from when I was a young girl. I had a deep wound in my heart because of him. He hated me. He only hated me among the family. He used to scold and hit me.

Now, here was my father asking for forgiveness, "Bong-Nyo, I have done many bad things. I am very sorry. I have sinned against you many times. I have no words to make it up. The punishment is fair and I deserve to be tormented. I cannot disagree with the judgment. But why are you here? Why are you visiting hell so frequently?" When my father finished speaking, the creature began to hack at and chop off his arms and legs without mercy. As he screamed, I turned away. I could not look. I asked the Lord, "Lord, please, I want to leave this place."

FINANCIAL BLESSING ON MY FAMILY

Sister Baek, Bong-Nyo: I prayed, "Lord, why haven't You kept Your promise to financially bless us? You broke Your promise. Look at us. Look at the condition we are in. When we pray, we pray in the cold because we cannot afford heat. While we pray, we shiver, and we constantly have to rub our hands together to keep warm. In most cases, it is below ten degrees. I do not understand why You have not blessed us. My family of four resides at the pastor's home, and even he is struggling financially. They have nothing to eat except rice and kimchee. Why have You not blessed us?"

I continued praying, "Both families are in extreme financial distress. The pastor's family does not have money and my family does not have money. We are struggling. How do You expect us to pray for long hours when we are hungry? You have given us the ability to enter into a deep spiritual realm when we pray. But we will not be able to continue if we are starving. Moreover, we are very cold. It is so cold. Why do You continually have me experience the hurt of watching others in torment in hell? I know how much it hurts when my body aches; however, I cannot imagine the pain they must be going through. When the church folks pray all night long, they are stiff and swollen from sitting in that position. Our bodies ache in pain and stiffness. Our bodies are not being conditioned normally. Praying all night long is very challenging. We do not have strong physical bodies because of the lack of proper food. Why do You let us continue like that? Lord, I cannot bear it anymore."

I cried over and over as I complained to the Lord. I resented my situation, which I described further in my prayers: "I worshiped evil spirits and lived as a fortune-teller for thirteen years. Take me into the burning flames of hell instead of my mother. It is I who wronged other people. I am responsible for many in hell; their blood is on my hands. Lord, You already know I was influenced by evil spirits. It was the evil spirits who got me to run away, abandoning my own children and becoming a fortune-teller. My mother accepted the responsibility and raised my children. Now she is in hell and in torment. It is not fair, and I cannot live with the guilt. Send me to hell and free my mother. Please!" I was babbling and complaining without first thinking. But the Lord was kindly listening and hearing every word. The Lord was truly patient with me. After my complaints, I looked at the Lord to observe His countenance.

I was expecting the Lord to give me an answer, but He stood in silence. He was gauging my countenance. There was a long pause, and then the Lord burst out laughing. Then He responded, "Bong-Nyo, I took and showed many people the experiences of hell. However, you are the first to complain about your financial needs while I showed you the torments of hell." The Lord laughed again. I felt ashamed as I listened to His kind words. I wanted to go hide somewhere.

I had been saved for only two months. My faith was new and immature. I was ignorant of the Lord's teaching. The Lord, with His warm words, began to gently speak, "I do not mind your complaints. We do not need to worry about anything. Let us move on. Now, look at this scene." I observed an animal moving in front of me. It was as large as a mountain. It was impossible for me to calculate the size of the beast. I could not determine what kind of beast it looked like. It resembled an alligator or a dragon. It had more than one hundred tails and the face of a human. It had about one hundred heads. When it opened its mouth, a long, string-like tongue endlessly came out. An old lady wearing a white dress stood next to the enormous beast. The beast had coiled her up with its tongue. I realized it was my mother.

The evil beast used its tongue to coil its victims. Once the victim entered its mouth, the beast would chew and swallow each person. I was intensely aggrieved. I wept and wept. The Lord watched. "Bong-Nyo, when you cry, I feel your pain. When your heart grieves, My heart grieves as well. When you are sad, I am sad. If your mother were still alive, I could have helped you. However, it is too late. If you want to complain and be angry, you may do so. I will be here to listen to your hurt. I know you are distressed. I desire for you to vent it all out," the Lord said to me.

I was ashamed and regretful of all my ignorant actions. I continued to weep. The Lord wanted me to look forward. As I lifted my head to look, I noticed a large black pot. Inside the pot was black boiling water. There was an awful odor all around. It smelled like mold from rotted food. My head began to pound, and I felt like vomiting from the smell. "Lord, what is it?" I asked, and the Lord answered, "It is a large pot of liquor. It is rotted with mold." The Lord wanted me to take a closer look. There was a large multitude of people lined up with evil spirits waiting to place them into the pot.

Pastor Kim's Father, Older Sister, and My Younger Brother in Hell

The words Jesus said to me brought sorrow to my heart. The Lord began to explain about the lined-up people and the pot. Among the multitudes of people were my younger brother, the pastor's father, and his older sister. They were lined up with the others waiting to be placed into the boiling pot. As I looked closer, I noticed my brother standing first in line and the pastor's father and older sister behind him. My brother saw me and began to cry out, "Sister, why have you come again?" I began to weep in distress, knowing he was first in line to enter the boiling pot.

I remembered how my brother died. While he was alive, he overdosed on poisonous pills. The memory made me squirm in discomfort. I remember how he cared about my relationship with my husband. He was so worried about our marriage. He said, "Sister, do not fight with your husband. How the world would be wonderful if both of you loved and lived in peace. Why do you two fight? Do you understand what I am trying to say to you? I will die before you, but I want you and your husband to live a happy, long life."

I attempted to communicate with my brother. In a loud voice, I cried out, "I am so sorry. I was not able to keep my promise. I divorced my husband and became a fortune-teller. I worshiped many evil spirits for many years. Because of my rebellion, my children paid the price and had a difficult life. Please forgive me, brother." However, he did not seem to be listening.

He continued to ask, "Sister, why do you continuously come here?" I replied, "Because Jesus keeps bringing me here. A pastor, Kim, Yong-Doo, evangelized to me one day, and I accepted Jesus and became a Christian. When I pray for long hours, the Lord visits me and takes me to hell. He has chosen me to show the realities of hell. I attend a church, it's called The Lord's Church. The pastor asked me to look for his father and older sister if I ever visited hell. By God's grace, I am able to meet all of you. I did not expect to see the pastor's father, older sister, and you all in one place."

When I had finished speaking, the evil creature guarding this domain appeared and shouted, "Stand straight in line." Everyone in line became nervous and tense. From nowhere, my father and mother appeared and were lined up with the pastor's father, sister, and my brother. As I looked inside the pot, rotten, dark water was intensely boiling. Just like a storm, I observed lightening striking from inside the pot with roars of thunder. The creature began to throw my father, mother, and younger brother into the boiling pot.

When I heard my parents and brother scream in pain, I became shocked and cried out, "Lord, why is this place so miserable?" The Lord replied, "This place is for the alcoholics who are cursed. Those who had not repented and had not accepted Jesus Christ will eventually enter the pot at least once." The lined-up people were thrown into the pot rapidly. Their screams echoed and reached the skies of hell. When the people entered the pot, their flesh disintegrated instantly. If some people were able to swim to the top, the evil creature would quickly club them on the head with an iron bar. The people were prevented from rising to the top of the boiling water. All the people were screaming for help.

The Lord waved at me to get my attention. He pointed at some people and commanded me to look closer. I saw two people standing. One was an old man who looked liked our pastor. The other person was a beautiful young lady. The older man was crying out the pastor's name. The pastor had told me he had seven siblings—five brothers, and two sisters. His older sister had died from illness at a young age. She was living in another city away from the pastor. The pastor looked just like his father. They could almost pass as twins.

The older man began to shout, "Yong-Doo. Where is my son?" The Lord advised me that He had already explained to him about the pastor. "Yong-Doo, where are you?" I asked the Lord, "Lord, why is the pastor's father here?" The Lord replied, "He sinned very much and was abusive to his wife. He loved to drink. Alcohol was his idol. His alcoholism affected his work, and he neglected his children. His children had a difficult life. As a result, he will taste and be tormented in this rotten liquor forever."

The pastor's father continued to shout, "Yong-Doo. Where did you go? I heard you had become a pastor. How was it possible for you to become a pastor? Why are you not visiting me in hell? Why has someone else come take your place?" The Lord replied to him, "Your son has become a pastor, and he is preaching the gospel." The pastor's father turned to me so I therefore introduced myself.

"Hello, I was a fortune-teller worshiping evil spirits. I got into an accident and ended up in the hospital. The pastor was evangelizing to the patients at the hospital, and I was one of the ones he evangelized. I accepted the Lord at that moment. Our church is located on the west side of Incheon. It is called The Lord's Church. The pastor is very faithful and dedicated. We pray daily; we pray all through the night. The Lord visits us, and this is how we have come here. I attend the church as well. The pastor is worried that you may be in hell. He was apprehensive that both you and his older sister were in hell. He asked me if I visited hell if I would look for you and his sister. He wished that I would have an opportunity to speak with you."

The pastor's father replied, "Oh, I see. But I do not understand how he has become a pastor. When he was a child, he was the most stubborn among my children. When I asked him to do something, he would never listen or obey. How is he qualified to become a pastor? Whenever I gave him money to buy me liquor, he would come back home very late. I cannot comprehend how he qualifies to become a pastor. If he is a pastor, why is he not visiting me here in hell? He should rescue me immediately."

I continued to converse with the pastor's father, "My pastor is praying fervently and passionately for the congregation's spiritual awakening. He prays for long hours and prays all through the night until morning. Whenever he prays, there are many evil spirits attacking him and the congregation. They attempt to stop us from praying and receiving the spiritual awakening. The pastor fights and continuously casts out evil spirits with all his strength. His prayers are powerful and intense." As the pastor's father cried, he spoke to me and said, "If I were still alive, I would listen to my son and accept the Lord as my Savior. I would attend church obediently. I would then be able to enter heaven. Oh, it is too late now. What can I do? Yong-Doo, my son, I wish I could see your face one more time." He was in such distress and sorrow.

The pastor resembled his father very closely. However, the pastor's father was taller and heavy-set. The pastor's father began to shout again, "Oh, I have done many terrible things. I wished my wife had accepted Jesus Christ as her Savior and Lord. She could then enter heaven. When I was on Earth I gambled and drank all day. I never took care of my family. I did not take care of their basic necessities. My wife labored all day to feed our children. I am responsible for her difficult life. The sins I had committed are being paid back. I deserved to be cursed. Please, when you go back to the world, tell my youngest son to continue to attend church. Tell him to be faithful to the Lord and believe." He also asked me to tell his sons not to attend church in vain. They should keep Sundays holy, repent sincerely, and walk with the Lord faithfully as a Christian.

The pastor's father spoke through tears. He was only able to speak because Jesus allowed it. The pastor's father said, "I am in hell and tormented. Hell is the final end, an endless torment. It is hopeless. Please evangelize to your brothers, sisters, and relatives so that they may have a chance to go to heaven."

Behind the pastor's father was a young lady. She had a pale white face. She was very beautiful. She was the pastor's older sister. With tears in her eyes, she began to speak, "My lovely sisters and brothers, please tell them to accept the Lord Jesus as Savior. Tell them to be obedient to the Lord so that they may go to heaven. My poor mother, I want to say I am sorry for hurting her. I miss her so much. My mother had a difficult and miserable life. I want my mother to go to heaven at any cost. Please tell them my message. I committed so many sins." As the pastor's sister spoke, a large centipede appeared. The grotesque looking creature had large round eyes and was preparing to devour its victims. The pastor's sister cried out, "My poor mother, my poor brothers and sisters. I have sowed so many wrong deeds." In front of Jesus, she cried and repented. However, the evil creature shouted, "You—repenting is only available while you are alive on Earth. Not here." The creature cursed her.

The pastor's sister had long, straight hair with baby-soft skin. The demon said, "You must have been very popular when you were alive." The centipede was preparing to devour her but was waiting for the proper opportunity to attack. The centipede drew close to the pastor's sister and coiled around her body and head. The centipede was very large and had thousands of legs. It used its body to torture, and it continuously stung its victims with its sharp teeth.

The centipede stung the pastor's sister, and her face turned pale blue. The poison began to spread all throughout her body. She looked terrible, and her appearance became appalling.

The pastor's father was thrown into the pot of the rotten liquor. The centipede was coiling around the older sister. Both of them still had the ability to speak. "My mother must be diligently working hard despite the harsh, cold weather. Please tell my mother to believe in Jesus Christ so that she may be saved. I do not have any feelings for my father. My father is responsible for my mother's difficult life. He never worked to feed his children. He spent his time at the bars. Miss, please warn my family on Earth. I feel sorry for my little brothers, sisters, and mother. I especially feel sorry for my mother. My little brothers and sisters probably have their own families now. My mother must be alone. My heart is heavy for her. My brothers and sisters are probably selfish and not taking care of her," she wailed out loud. I cried as well. I wanted to hold her and cry together. However, the Lord warned me not to get too close to them, and I could not even touch them. Therefore, from a distance, I pretended to hug her.

THE CROSSES IN HELL'S SKY

We said our good-byes to the pastor's father and older sister. The Lord then took me to the next place of torment. I wondered to myself, "Where will the Lord take me this time?" I followed the Lord and held His hand. I was uneasy and anxious about the next place.

We walked for a while and then the Lord raised and waved His hand to the sky. As I looked up at hell's sky, I was astonished at what I witnessed. There were multitudes of people filling the sky of hell. They were all hanging on a cross. There were so many people I could not see the sky very clearly. I was amazed at how many people were hanging on the cross in the air. I could not describe what I was witnessing. I did not have the words to express myself.

The multitudes of people were paired up together. Each person on a cross was facing another. Each person was nailed to a cross. The crosses were made out of wood. Jesus wanted me to get a closer look. There were many people of different ethnicities. As I observed closer, each person was crucified like the Lord Jesus had been. Large nails were pierced into their hands, and their feet were on top of one another and nailed. Sharp-thorned stems of ivy were coiled around their necks.

As each pair faced each other, numerous insects with thorns covered their bodies. Strangely, people continued to murmur without ceasing. As I watched in shock, I asked the Lord, "Lord, this is a horrible place. What kind of sin have they committed to be tormented here?"

ABSENTMINDED (CARNAL) BELIEVERS

After I had asked the question, I realized what sins they had committed. However, the Lord began to explain, and His tone turned to anger, "These are people who attended church regularly. They even took their Bibles to church. But they worshiped and prayed in vain. They were imposters. They were hypocrites. Outside church, they were drunkards and smokers. They did not keep the Sabbath. After church services, they would also enjoy leisure activities, such as mountain climbing and so forth. Some of these people were loan sharks. They would lend money and charge very high interest rates. They became wealthy charging high interest rates. Many families were not able to keep up with their interest rates and became bankrupt. Families were broken up due to financial stress. Their heart and actions were worldly, even though their words claimed faith. If they would have walked in faith with all their heart and strength, they would have entered heaven. They could not be born again due to their unfaithfulness. They were not born again, either with water or the Holy Spirit. They followed tradition rather than God. Their worldly activities were more important and took precedence over God. Their deeds did not reflect true faith. They served with halfhearted faith."

Once the Lord finished explaining, the creature loudly interrupted, speaking to the condemned people, "Whenever I see you, it pleases me. When you were on Earth, you posed as Christians. However, your faith was phony. I was the one who deceived you. I will show you what the price is for your unfaithfulness." The creature then gave a hand signal, and many types of insects, big and small, began to attack the people hanging within the sky. The insects began to crawl up from the peoples' feet. All the insects had two horns. I saw some of the insects gnawing at the people's feet, and the bones began to appear as the peoples' flesh was torn. As the insects worked their way up the peoples' heads, they would gnaw their way into their brains. The peoples' bodies began to melt, and some black liquid would hemorrhage out of them.

The creature commanded the people to repeat what he would say. The creature held an iron bar ready to strike the people. The people, in fear, would repeatedly shout in a loud voice whatever he commanded.

The people shouted in pain as black liquid hemorrhaged out of their bodies. They attempted to endure the pain of the nails that were hammered into their hands and feet. They had to endure the pain of the thorns around their necks and the pain of insects eating their flesh and bones. Moreover, they had to repeat the creature's command with a loud voice. It was the torment of torment.

If their voices were not loud enough, the evil creatures would all come together and beat the people unmercifully and throw them into the fire. The people would rather hang on the cross than be thrown in the burning fire of hell. The burning fire was the most dreadful place for them. They all appeared as though they were going insane. The insects ate into their bodies, and water from their dead bodies fell to the ground of hell. Puddles began to form from all the water. Eventually, the insects ate their flesh and their bones. Their bodies became dust and fell into the puddles of water on the ground of hell.

Once their dust fell into the filthy water, they became human form again with all their flesh and bones intact. The evil creatures would take them and nail them on to the cross. The thorny stems of ivy would then be placed around their necks. The Lord told me that this procedure will be repeated over and over for eternity. The Lord was very adamant and clear about His warning. He then said for me to look at the people who believed in vain. His explanation was a warning.

God's Church in Heaven

As I was shaking uncontrollably from fear, the Lord gently spoke to me, "Bong-Nyo, you are frightened. It is enough for today, let us go. Bong-Nyo, you have witnessed your family in torment. It has been a great deal to handle. You have cried very much. I wish to comfort and cheer you up. When we reach heaven and enter the church, I want you to pray and watch the worship." As soon as the Lord held my hand, the world of sorrow and tears were behind us. We were up in the bright shining sky of heaven.

Heaven's world is truly fantastic. With the Lord holding my hand, we were already inside God's heavenly church. I had heard about God's church, but now I had the honor of actually being there.

God's church in heaven is shining with glorious bright light and the light beams covered all of heaven's sky. The temple was enormous. It was impossible for me to imagine the size of the church. I could not tell if there was a second or third level. I was only able to view the first floor. The floor of the temple was made of solid gold. The altar was made of gold. In fact, everything was made of gold.

There were multitudes of saints worshiping. Moreover, many angels with wings were joining the saints in the service. The Lord began to preach, "I have brought Sister Baek, Bong-Nyo from the Earth. But before we came here, I had showed her hell. While we were in hell, Sister Baek, Bong-Nyo experienced and witnessed her family in torment. She cried very much and was shocked from observing the trauma. Therefore, I want all the angels here to comfort her. At first, I intended to show her her pastor's his father and older sister. However, she had to meet her family first. Angels, go to Sister Baek, Bong-Nyo and comfort her."

Suddenly, I heard familiar music play from all directions. I recognized that it was the song we often sing at our church. It is called "Baptize with the Holy Spirit." I observed a group of angels attending the service. It appeared that they had just finished their tasks on Earth. Those angels were ranked lower than other angels. Jesus commanded once again in a loud voice from the altar, "All saints, look at my body. I was crucified on the cross. I poured out my blood and died for you." The moment He spoke, He was hanging on the cross, which was standing on the altar. A bright golden beam of light shined on to the cross. I felt a warm sensation coming over my body as I sat on the church chair. Many angels came to me and spoke sweet, comforting words. I was very happy.

The Lord was attempting to comfort my sorrowful heart. How could the Lord try that hard and give attention to a person who is the lowest of the low? I was just a sinner and I have only been attending the church for two months. I have sinned so much that all I have been doing is repenting. I was only a filthy sinner, and I pray with tears.

DAY FIFTEEN

My brethren, count it all joy when ye fall into divers temptations; Knowing this, that the trying of your faith
worketh patience. But let patience have her perfect work,
that ye may be perfect and entire, wanting nothing.

—JAMES 1:2–4

Baek, Bong-Nyo: After Sunday service, the church family had lunch
at the pastor's house. It had been a while since we gathered with the
Sunday congregation for a lunch event. We had a good time conversing
about our prayers during the night. I tried to persuade the deaconess,
Shin Sung Kyung, to come and join our evening prayers. Deaconess
Shin is in her early thirties and has a calm and introverted personality.
I thought to myself, "If Shin attends night prayers and experiences the
fire of the Holy Spirit, which manifests through the night, I wonder
how she is going to be changed." I was very curious as to how she
would turn out. Whenever I attend nighttime services, I often feel like
I am on another planet because God manifests Himself so strongly.
We are filled with the Holy Spirit and His grace.

I worshiped idols until I was saved. I had never met Jesus. Now I
am experiencing all of it in real life at The Lord's Church. During my
experiences, I often thought, "How can these things happen?" I was
often curious about the experiences I was having. I said these things
must have been happening because I had worshiped and serviced
evil spirits. I often doubted my experiences. However, whenever I
doubted, the Lord would provide an answer. He always kindly gave
me answers like, "Bong-Nyo, you will never know how much I love

you. You decided to follow and believe in Me; therefore, I will forget your previous transgressions. I will always protect you in a special way." He then blessed me.

I had attended church once or twice in my life. The church I had attended was a megachurch. I had never experienced any of these events before. But now, within a small church, I am encountering these events. I often thought and worried that I was attending a cult group. But the Lord explained it clearly, "Pastor Kim and his wife, Kang, Hyun-Ja, have been praying fervently and earnestly. It did not matter whether they had a congregation or not. It did not matter if there was tribulation or not. They never had any doubt in Me. This is why I had used Pastor Kim to evangelize to you."

What I realized was that the pastor and his wife had always held prayer meetings all night long. Jesus was very impressed with their dedication and had led me to The Lord's Church. I received the gift of tongues on the very first night of services. At that time, I was ignorant of spiritual gifts and wondered how someone like me could have received such a gift. Now, one or two hours of prayer does not satisfy my soul. I can easily pray for three or four hours. In fact, I often pray for seven hours straight.

After fifteen days of dedicated prayer meetings, the Lord generously provided an opportunity for the Deaconess Shin to accompany us. At that night's service and prayer meeting, the Deaconess Shin was going to be joining us, which made me jump for joy. Our church only constitutes a few members, but when Sunday arrives we attend with all of our family members. We gather together joyfully to talk about our experiences in meeting Jesus. Everyone gets excited.

When we come to worship, the services are fantastic, as Jesus appears. Multitudes of angels come from heaven to dance with us. They get busy to gather incense—the prayers of saints to present before God. The angels are also busy meticulously recording the details of the service. It includes the behavior of people and the scenes. I was not the only person able to witness the events. Those who were spiritually awakened had the opportunity to clearly observe: Joo-Eun,

Haak-Sung, and Yoo-Kyung were watching the amazing events. As they watched, they clapped in amazement.

SATAN USING TV AND COMPUTERS TO PUT PEOPLE IN BONDAGE

Kim, Joo-Eun: While I was fervently praying, a vision appeared before me. It was a person in his home. I was able to visualize it clearly. The person was a man lying on his side and watching TV. As he was watching TV, a grotesque-looking evil spirit came forth from the TV and entered his body. The person had not realized the spiritual effects of watching TV.

My vision switched over to another scene. It was a room with many computers; it was an Internet café. The Internet café provided numerous computers where people rented time to surf the Internet or play games twenty-four hours a day, seven days a week. The place was packed with many gamers. They were playing games all night long. A particular man came to my vision. This man was mesmerized, and all his attention was on his Internet game. He must have been playing for hours, his eyes red and bloodshot. Suddenly, an evil spirit in the form of a skeleton came forth from the computer screen and entered the man's body. With the evil spirit in him, he became more addicted and played feverously. What I observed had shocked me. "Wow, how could that have happened?" I asked myself. "I also enjoy computers and surfing the Internet, but now I will not fall victim to it," I decided. I made my decision to be more cautious with what I watch and do on the Internet.

I returned to praying in tongues. As I was praying, an evil spirit in the shape of a half-moon appeared. It usually was an evil spirit in the form of a crescent moon, but now it was another spirit. The half-moon-shaped spirit had an eye within its eye. Its inner eye was black in color. It somehow had a head shaped as a skull. It did not have any lips, but it had teeth, which would grind together. I shouted, "In the name of Jesus Christ, depart from me." It did not dare to draw closer to me.

With an agitated voice, it said, "Let me go to the Internet café." I saw a vision of this evil spirit heading toward the Internet café. The Internet café became vivid in my sight. I saw a man intensely playing his game. He appeared addicted to the game. The evil spirit said, "Since you are so consumed with the games, I will enter your body." It then entered the body of the person. I saw numerous evil spirits approaching the people to harass them. The evil spirits were spirits of addiction. Some saints fell into this trap. They spent less time in prayer and more time with computers. There were dedicated church folks who had fallen into the addiction of the Internet and TV. As a result, their church attendance and spiritual life were compromised. The evil spirits were responsible for enticing the people to fall in love with TV and/or computers and the Internet. I had witnessed the spiritual consequences of TV and the Internet. These people became blind and did not realize that evil spirits were responsible for their addictions and actions. People fell into deeper traps.

I saw another vision. As soon as people turned on their television, evil spirits in the form of skeletons flew out of the TVs. They had the wings of bats and flapped out of TVs to enter their victims' bodies. I was very frightened and shocked. I said to myself, "Now I see how these evil spirits work. Whenever I have to make decision or do anything, I will ask the Lord from this point on." I was convicted with this decision.

Satan Does Not Let Us Pray in Peace

While I shouted in prayer, an evil spirit with long, sharp teeth resembling a shark's appeared. The evil spirit had long hair and an eerie, wicked laugh. I was very frightened, and as a result I opened my eyes during prayer several times. However, I closed my eyes and began to pray. I then heard a terrifying, horrid sound. The sound gave me goose bumps all over my body. I felt like running to the altar next to the pastor. I knew the pastor was praying, and I did not want to interrupt him. Therefore, I decided to be patient and continue praying. I shouted with all my strength, and the evil spirit departed.

I was able to compose myself and began to pray again. A crescent moon-shaped evil spirit drew toward me, but I was able to rebuke it immediately. As I wrestled with the evil spirit, the Lord appeared and called my name, "Joo-Eun, I will take you to heaven and show you several places tomorrow night." I replied, "Lord, I have not seen enough of hell. I wish You would take me to hell again." I began to cry. The Lord said, "Joo-Eun, when you cry during your prayer, My heart hurts," and the Lord cried with me.

After Jesus departed, I composed myself and began to pray. As I continued to pray, an evil spirit with a large head approached me. The spirit had three eyes on its forehead, a horn on its head, and a mouth. It had a small body. As it drew closer to me, it opened and closed its mouth as though it wanted to gnaw at me. It looked very ugly with its mouth open. A sticky liquid drooled from the mouth of the spirit. It had menacing, large teeth resembling a crocodile's. I shouted, "In the name of Jesus, filthy evil spirit, depart." As I shouted, it transformed into a man dressed in black. It looked like something from out of an old horror film, but I cast it out in Jesus's name.

This time, another evil spirit appeared before me in the form of a lion. It was very frightening, and I began to shake. The lion had a large face and head with a lot of fur around the neck. Its teeth and claws were frightening. However, I kept on praying. The lion drew closer to me and roared. It took the posture of devouring me. The evil spirit said, "I will take you down to the chambers of hell." I shouted, "What are you talking about? You filthy evil spirit, in the name of Jesus Christ, depart." It then departed.

I was relieved once the evil spirit departed, but without any rest, another evil spirit appeared. I said to myself, "Why are there so many evil spirits appearing today?" This particular evil spirit came in the form of two eyes. The pair of eyes had two legs attached to it. It walked in an amusing manner. I laughed at it as it reminded me of a duck walking. The evil spirit angrily shouted, "Why are you laughing at me?" I answered, "Because you look amusing. Is that wrong?" It then said to me, "Do not laugh."

The evil spirit responded by using my nickname, "Hey, Freckles. You are Freckles, right? Do not laugh, Freckles." It was making fun of me. I shouted, "You filthy evil spirit. Jesus gave me that nickname for me. He calls me that because He adores me. How dare you call me by my nickname. Jesus gave me that special name. You useless, filthy evil spirit. You ugly-looking evil spirit. In the name of Jesus, depart from me." It then departed.

I felt victorious and was having fun at the same time. As I prayed, I could not help but smile. Within a short time, I heard the sound of a woman walking. It was the sound of heels tapping on cement. It was an evil spirit disguised as a young woman in a white dress. I was the most afraid of this spirit. She always appeared with long, straight hair and a white dress. Her eyes were long and slender as blood dripped down from them. She had fangs like Dracula's, with blood drizzling down her mouth.

As I became more frightened, she drew closer to me. She came face-to-face with me and then she opened her mouth wide. Out of fear, I opened my eyes. Whenever I open my eyes, I see the other saints praying.

When I closed my eyes to pray, I would see evil spirits. As a result, I would pray next to my mother or pastor. However, it did not help, because when I closed my eyes during prayers, I was still alone. The evil spirits would not leave me alone.

I closed my eyes again and began to pray in tongues. As I prayed, the evil spirit with the white dress stared at me with a wicked look. It was distracting me from praying. I called upon the Lord's name, "Lord, I am very scared. Please help me." The evil spirit with the white dress departed as it expressed bitterness in its face.

Relieved, I thought to myself, "It should be all right now." I therefore began to pray again. Soon after, the evil spirit that Sister Baek, Bong-Nyo described appeared. It was very ugly. It had the face of a goblin with many heads. The face and head were covered with eyes, and it had several hands and legs. I reacted to its appearance and shouted, "You filthy evil spirit. I abhor your appearance. In the name of Jesus, depart." It then departed. By then I was very tired from casting out so many evil spirits that day.

Due to the lack of strength, I could not raise my arms any longer. Then my head fell forward. As a result, my whole body fell flat to the floor during prayer time. I do not remember how the prayer meeting ended. I think I prayed for about four hours. After we had finished the prayer meeting, we gathered to eat rice balls.

As I was eating, Sister Baek, Bong-Nyo described what she had seen. When I was passed out, Jesus came down with two angels and sat next to me. He stroked my hair and said He had come to take me to heaven. Jesus said, "Joo-Eun, I have come to take you to heaven and show you many places, but you have fallen onto the floor due to your tiredness. Get up, Joo-Eun. Get up and let us go to heaven together," He said to me. Sister Baek, Bong-Nyo told me that I was not responding. As soon as I heard what had happened, I was disappointed. I thought to myself, "Why did the Lord come when I was passed out? He should have come a little earlier." My heart was troubled, and I was quite disappointed. Tears began to run from my eyes.

HAAK-SUNG DANCES WITH JESUS

Lee, Haak-Sung: While I was praying in tongues, several evil spirits began to attack me, as usual. The first one looked like a large bullfrog. It was very chubby. It began to hop toward me. The frog had no color. It was almost transparent. It had three eyes lined in a row with black spots all over its back. The appearance was unpleasant. I commanded it to leave my presence, and I was able to cast it out in Jesus' name.

The second evil spirit appeared with a human face. Half of its face was severely burned, and it had only one eye due to the burn. The evil spirit had the ears of a donkey with another small ear within the donkey ear. It had no hands and was walking barefoot. It walked toward me as it showed its menacing teeth, which reminded me of

Dracula. I was frightened by the unusual, grotesque appearance and called upon the name of the Lord. As I called the Lord's name, He appeared wearing a crown of thorns.

The evil spirit fled as the Lord appeared. Jesus approached me, and I noticed He was bleeding. He stood in silence and bled in front of me. I could not imagine the amount of blood that the Lord was losing. The blood hemorrhaged from all sides of His head. It appeared endless. I began to cry and asked the Lord, "Jesus, what should I do? Jesus, You died for me." I sobbed profusely as I cried out to the Lord. The Lord laid His hands out toward me to show me His wrists. I saw the holes where the nails had pierced him and from which His blood was streaming out.

As I sobbed profusely, the Lord commanded me to dance with Him. I had never danced before, but I knew I must obey His requests. I was apprehensive and not in any mood to dance. I was attempting to gather myself from bawling like a baby. The tears streamed endlessly down my face. However, the Lord held my hand, and as He still bled, we danced. We danced without saying any words, and I followed His lead.

I followed the Lord and did not know how I was dancing. The Lord said, "Haak-Sung, you did a good job of evangelizing today. You also do a very good job in cleaning the church." He appeared very proud of my efforts and continued to compliment me, "My Haak-Sung, as you evangelized, you led and took care of the little brothers and sisters. The weather was very cold, but you overcame those obstacles. You did a good job. I am very proud of you." He then gave me a hug.

Once Jesus left, four evil spirits appeared and attacked me all at once. The first evil spirit had the form of a skeleton. The bones all separated from their joints and began to dance. The second evil spirit was the same one from before Jesus appeared, the human with the burnt face. It attempted to distract my prayer as it spoke, "Do not pray. Stop. You cannot pray." The third evil spirit appeared, and it had long hair dyed yellow. It tried to confuse and distract me by moving rapidly side to side. It moved in front of my eyes. Another spirit in the form of a hand attempted to interrupt my prayer by dancing and moving along the church walls and ceiling. All the evil spirits attempted to distract my prayer. I concentrated with all my strength not to lose focus, and I shouted with my heart. I powerfully called upon the name of Jesus in my prayer. As a result, all the evil spirits fled.

ALCOHOLICS IN HELL
TORMENTED IN A LARGE BOILING POT

After I had cast out the evil spirits, Jesus appeared. With a smile, He said, "Haak-Sung, we have places to visit. Let us now go together." As soon as He held my hand, we were in hell instantly. I then saw an enormous heated black pot. When I looked inside the pot, I saw boiling water with hot steam rising. It appeared as though the water had being boiling for some time.

Jesus commanded me to take a closer look. I realized there were multitudes of people screaming and shouting in pain from the boiling water. Their screams echoed as I drew closer. Among the people, a particular man caught my attention. He raised a hand toward me and called my name, "Haak-Sung, get me out of here. It is very hot." As I turned toward the man, I realized it was my cousin. He tried to grab me for help. The creature assigned to this place quickly flew to the pot and mercilessly beat my cousin with a club, drawing him back into the pot. The creature appeared to be a bat.

The evil spirit or creature had a long, huge horn on its forehead. This place was filled with evil spirits walking and flying in all directions. It appeared as though there were countless creatures. They looked like dragons and flying snakes as I noticed their wings spread out. Jesus said to me, "Haak-Sung, do not be afraid. The numerous evil spirits cannot harm you as long as I am here to protect you."

The evil spirits glanced at us as they passed by. The Lord said, "This is a place called the torment of the boiling pot. It is a place for alcoholics and people addicted to smoking." As the people entered the boiling water, their flesh disintegrated. Strangely, there was fire inside the boiling water. As I watched, the Lord decided to leave and gestured to me that it was time to go. I said, "Amen." Before a second had passed, we were already back in church.

The Devil's Continuous Appearance

Lee, Yoo-Kyung: While I was praying, the evil spirit in the form of a basketball player that brother Haak-Sung described appeared. It spoke to me as it dribbled its head, "Would you like to play a round of basketball with me?" I replied, "You filthy evil spirit, in the name of Jesus Christ, depart." I had cast it out. Soon after, another evil spirit appeared. This evil spirit resembled a cartoon character on television. Half of its face was human and the other half was a mask. This evil spirit had a horn on its head. As usual, I cast it out in Jesus name.

Another evil spirit appeared and called me by the nickname that Jesus had given me. It harassed me with a wicked laugh, saying, "Miss Moe." I rebuked it, "That nickname was given to me by Jesus. How dare you call me by my nickname." The evil spirit replied with a wicked giggle, "I am able to hear everything you speak." I angrily said, "You filthy spirit. In the name of Jesus, depart."

After the evil spirit departed, another one took its place. This time, the evil spirit came in the form of a human hand, which Brother Haak-Sung encountered. It tried to frighten me by moving randomly around me. Then another evil spirit appeared. It was the same basketball player spirit. It begged me to play a game. "Do you not know how fun it is to play basketball?" it asked. "Hurry, let us play." It continued to annoy me. I shook my head and shouted, "No, no." I then cast it out in Jesus' name.

Soon after, Jesus appeared wearing a bright, shining garment. Jesus held my hand and said, "Yoo-Kyung, let us go to heaven." As we arrived in heaven, the angels greeted us as usual. Jesus always took me to the room filled with many books. He desired for me to explore and read the enormous collection of books. I observed many subjects and different varieties of books, which were elegantly stored on shelves. There were so many books I could not stop observing the different subjects. The books were made out of gold. I always loved coming into this room to visit. As I touched and explored the countless books, the Lord said, "Yoo-Kyung, let us go to hell now." I responded with resistance. "No, I do not want to go. I do not wish to see hell." However, the Lord gently led me and said that He had a certain place I needed to see. Jesus said, "I will always be with you. Do not worry." As He tightly held my hand, we traveled to hell.

THE ETERNAL SUFFERING OF HELL

It always amazed me how we instantly traveled to one place to another. As long as I held the Lord's hand, I was either in heaven, hell, or the church within less than a second. The Lord and I stood at the center of hell. The Lord took me to view the most dreadful scene. I dreaded the scene of my grandmother in torment.

I saw my grandmother in a place where the flames of fire burned the highest. Although I stood at a distance, I could still sense the heat from the fire. My grandmother stood next to a frying pan. The enormous frying pan was hot. Large flames of red and blue illuminated the area. I saw multitudes of people being fried with oil. I heard their awful screams. I saw the fear on the faces of those waiting in line to be fried. All of them shook hysterically as they stepped forward.

My grandmother was first in line. She cried out in fear. The creature assigned to the pan lifted her and threw her into the frying pan. Within a second, she screamed, "Ahh, it is so hot. Someone save me." I almost fainted as I heard the awful scream.

I saw multitudes of people frying in the pan with my grandmother. They were all crying out, "Save me, get me out of here. Help." After being tormented in the frying pan, they were thrown into the fire. The people were burned without end. They were burned eternally. The smell of burning flesh filled the air and the smoke rose high to the sky. It was difficult to see with all the smoke. The creature would then drag the victims out of the burning fire. As they were taken out of the fire, all their flesh would reappear and intact. I then saw a large snake appear, and it coiled my grandmother from her feet up to her neck. It began to tighten its grip.

As the snake tightened its grip on my grandmother, she shouted to me, "Yoo-Kyung, please ask Jesus to save me. I cannot take this anymore. Oh, I cannot bear the torment anymore." The snake then broke her neck. I shouted from the top of my lungs, "Grandma! Jesus, please do something. Father God." But the Lord said, "It is too late."

The belligerent creature threw my grandmother back into the frying pan. She appeared like a helpless lady without hope. However, once she was in the frying pan, she somehow gained enough strength to scream in pain. Her flesh disintegrated. The vicious cycle repeated over and over. Multitudes of people including my grandmother would regain their human form. They would then be thrown in the frying pan as their flesh disintegrated and only their bones would remain. The creature would take their skeleton out of the pan and the people would regain their form. Lastly, the snake would tightly coil its victims and break their necks.

Jesus said, "Hell is an eternal place of torment. Multitudes of people, including your grandmother, are in eternal torment. They will be tormented eternally through a vicious cycle." I then heard my grandmother scream to me, "Yoo-Kyung, do you not feel sorry for me? How can you just stand there and watch me tormented? I am pleading to you. Please save me. I cannot bear it anymore. It is too hot. Yoo-Kyung, please do something."

After her sorrowful plea, I began to cry boisterously. The Lord put His arms around me and comforted me. I shouted to the evil creature, "Creature, do not touch my grandmother. Do not torment her." However, my demands were in vain. The creature had countless heads and multiple hands and legs attached to all parts of its body. Jesus said, "Yoo-Kyung, you do not have to watch anymore." The Lord then led me to another place. As we left, my grandmother's screams faded away in the distance. When we arrived at our destination, I noticed three evil spirits dancing in joy.

They were unpleasant looking spirits. One of the evil spirits had an enormous head while another had a very small head. The third one had hair on the center of its head. The evil spirits were a distance away, but I could tell that they were speaking with foul language. I saw them run to their victims, and they unmercifully tore them up with their teeth. The Lord and I drew closer to get a better view.

I was shell-shocked and almost fainted. It was my grandmother again. I had previously seen her tormented in the frying pan. Now, I was seeing her again tormented by different evil spirits. The evil spirits cursed my grandmother, "You shall die. You shall die." They continued to curse her without rest. The evil spirits ran toward her and bit her ears off. My grandmother screamed in pain, "Ouch!" She jumped and stumbled as she held her hands over the side of her head. She tried to run and escape, but the evil spirits would block and bite her as she tried to pass them. I wanted to rebuke them, but I knew it would not be effective. I was heartbroken. I said to the Lord, "Jesus, this is so frightening." I was in terror. The Lord said, "Let us go now. We have seen enough for today." We then left hell.

Hell is a horrible and frightening place. I was relieved that I knew the Lord. However, streams of tears ran down my face as I reflected on my poor grandmother. Once I arrived back in our church, I began to pray. As I prayed, an evil spirit in the form of a skeleton appeared. The skull was covered with larvae. When I commanded it to leave in the Lord's name, the evil spirit departed.

While I fervently prayed, Jesus came back again and took me to heaven. Jesus had brought Yeh-Jee with Him. We then flew all over heaven and we arrived at heaven's ocean. The ocean of heaven is as clear as crystal. We played in the water, splashing and swimming. Many angels arrived and watched us play. They were amused as I noticed them laughing as they watched us. They must have enjoyed it. Yeh-Jee and I hung out together with the angels. We had lots of fun together. We sang many songs together.

The Lord gave my mother the nickname "Beautiful." She is a beautiful woman. He also gave my niece, Meena, the nickname "Crying baby."

My Nephew and
Brother-in-law Are in Hell

Baek, Bong-Nyo: As I praying in tongues, I saw two angels coming down from above. They came toward us. I asked them what the purpose was for their visiting us. They stated that they were commanded to bring sister Baek, Bong-Nyo from The Lord's Church. I was excited to hear this news. However, they had come to take me to hell. My joy was short-lived.

The angels and I walked along the road to hell. It was endless and dark. I was nervous and fearful and felt panicked. We walked for a long time. There were mushroom-shaped trees along the side of the road. But I soon found out that the trees were not mushrooms but humans dug into the ground. It was a shocking scene.

As I looked closer, I noticed something strange. They had human faces, but they had the body of a snake. Instead of feet, they had the end of a snake's tail. Their whole bodies were dug into the ground. As I continued to look, my heart raced and goose bumps ran down my body. "How can this be?" I asked myself. Their faces had a strange look. I did not have the words to explain it.

I did not notice that Jesus had arrived and was standing next to me. Jesus and I stood in front of the people who were cursed. They were pleading and sobbing to the Lord, "Lord, please return our normal bodies." As I watched, I suddenly heard someone calling my name. "Bong-Nyo, look over here. Here. Over Here." I recognized the voice. It was my brother-in-law who had died many years ago.

As I turned to where the voice was coming from, I noticed another man standing next to him. An electrical current was flowing next to the men. It appeared as though it was their turn to be thrown into the electrical current. My nephew and brother-in-law were pale blue as they spoke. They both called my name. I thought to myself, "What are they afraid of?" I did not see or notice any torment device or method. They were standing in an open field. However, as I looked closer to where they were standing, it was not a joke. Every single aspect of hell is frightening. Every place in hell is a place of misery, pain, and torment.

In a short time, lightning and thunder lit up the skies of hell. It sounded like the sky was being torn apart. Lightning struck near my nephew and brother-in-law.

We were startled by the lightning as it struck the ground and made us step back in fear. Within a second, a creature assigned to this place brought a man and lined him up behind my brother-in-law. As my brother-in-law shook in fear, he shouted, "Sister, what should I do? If I stand here, all my bones will scatter and my body will perish. Sister, please ask Jesus so that I am not sent there. Please. Oh, what am I going to do? Sister, I have committed so many abusive acts against your big sister. Please go and tell your big sister I apologize for the pain I had caused her. OK?"

My brother-in-law spent most of his life as a hunter, hunting birds. He loved to hunt. My sister had a difficult life. My sister was in pain that cannot be described. On one occasion, he demanded my sister to hastily prepare a meal before his hunting trip. He also asked her to prepare a lunch bag to take on his trip. My sister urgently went to the kitchen and began to prepare the meal and lunch. While she was in the kitchen, he had overdosed on poison that was used for hunting birds. He had committed suicide.

Now he is in hell with no turning back. He begged me to give the message to my sister. He said that he was very sorry for the mistakes he had made. He then asked me to tell my sister and his daughter to believe in Jesus at any cost. Moreover, he asked me to tell them to pray without ceasing. He desired very much for them to be saved.

The man standing next to my brother-in-law was my nephew. He worked on a ship as a crewmember. He worked on a fishing boat. The work was very tough. His coworkers harassed and beat him. He was not given the opportunity to rest much during work. He had an illness and died. He shouted to me, "Auntie, I thought there was no afterlife and I would just sleep in peace. But I ended up in this scary place. They said I will be tormented for eternality. What am I going to do? Auntie, please save me. Do something." He was sobbing profusely.

Lightning and thunder struck near them, and both of them were thrown down into the ground. They shouted, "Save me." However, the lightning struck them and they were turned into ashes. I began to cry. The angels that were with me attempted to comfort me, but I sobbed hysterically. I begged and pleaded to the Lord, "Lord, I came to this place to see my parents and my younger brother in torment. As a result, I cry all day long and my heart and body are weak. I am not able to move because of my weakened condition. Why are You showing me this again? How could You show me such torment? Lord, I cannot watch anymore. I cannot bear it. I cannot be patient with it anymore."

THE PAIN OF WATCHING FAMILY MEMBERS IN TERRIBLE TORMENT

As I cried out in pain watching my family members in torment, the Lord held my hand. Jesus once again grabbed my hand and brought me to the place where the enormous evil creature resided. I could not see the end of the head of the creature; the size of the creature was gigantic. I was able to see all kinds of animals inside the giant's body. I could hear the animals crying. There were wolves, cats, tigers, lions, and horses, among many others. These wild animals were endlessly growling. When the creature opened its mouth, I saw another mouth inside the mouth and another mouth within that mouth. It went on continuously. I estimated that there were about seventy to one hundred mouths. The creature also had seventy to one hundred separate heads. The creature was black. It had a long tongue and teeth like a shark. There were multitudes of people sucked into the mouth of the creature. I saw my mother among the multitude of people.

I instantly felt pain as the eyes of my mother and mine met. My mother pleaded to me to save her. I can never forget her expression or the way she stared at me. How can I ever erase that from my memory? She pleaded with me, "Bong-Nyo, please save me. I told you not to come here. What is the purpose for you to come? If you were to come again, you should have asked the Lord to take me out of here instead of just watching and crying. Did you just come to see me in torment?" As she cried, she was quickly sucked into the mouth of the creature.

While I unconsciously cried, the scene of my little brother committing suicide reappeared as a vision. I could hear his voice saying to me, "Sister, I am having terrible stomach pains. Please save me, sister. The pain in my stomach is unbearable." While my brother cried out in pain, I was helpless and could not do anything. With anger, I pleaded to the Lord, "Why Lord? Why do You continuously take me to hell and let me experience unbearable pain? My mother, little brother, father, my brother-in-law, and my nephew are all cursed and in torment. Jesus, how could You do this to me? I cry every day and my body has weakened due to the visitations of hell. Why don't You take Pastor Kim and show him heaven and hell? He prays for many hours, more than I do. It is he who desires to visit heaven or hell. Why have you chosen me to experience the pain of watching loved ones in torment?" Jesus stood silent. The Lord showed me more tormented places.

During the middle of the prayer meeting, we had a visitor. She was the wife of a pastor from another church. Moreover, she and her husband were close friends of Pastor Kim. She said she had come again because she was so blessed by the previous prayer meeting she had attended. Furthermore, she had some questions and wanted to be consulted in regard to spiritual issues. Our prayer meeting ended earlier due to our unexpected guest. Once their discussion was over, a ride was given to the guest by our pastor. We then began a second prayer service.

While I was praying in tongues, my family's torment in hell crossed my mind. I became tearful. The Lord returned once again. I pleaded to the Lord, "Lord, next time, please take the pastor instead of me. The pastor is more eligible to experience and write an accurate account." The Lord replied, "Very well. Be a little more patient. You have a little more to experience."

MEETING THE ARCHANGEL MICHAEL

As Jesus comforted me with warm words, He walked closer to me and said, "I will take you to heaven from here on. I will show you more of heaven. I will wipe your tears away. I know you have experienced much pain." He affectionately held my hand. As He held my hand, I was equipped with a bright, shining gown with wings. With my new wings, we flew into the cross standing at the altar.

Traveling to heaven is most exciting. After we flew through the Earth's atmosphere, we were passing through space. We passed through the multitudes of stars. We flew and traveled from galaxy to galaxy. We continued through a dark pit. As we passed through, we arrived at a place where two roads crossed. One road led to the left, which was hell. The right road led to heaven.

Jesus and I went right and came upon a bright, shining golden castle. Multitudes of angels came forward to greet and welcome us. From among the angles, the Lord introduced me to one particular angel. It was Michael, an angel that Pastor Kim spoke about during his sermon. Jesus said to Archangel Michael, "This saint has been a believer for only two months. This sheep has had the opportunity to experience and witness hell. She has been spiritually awakened during the appointed forty-day prayer meetings. She has experienced terrible shock in hell. She has witnessed the torment of her family today. I command you, Michael, to take her around heaven and show her the wonderful places. Comfort her as well."

Archangel Michael bowed his head and replied, "Yes, Lord." After that, Michael and I flew around different places in heaven. "Wow. It is incredible," I said to the angel. It was going to be impossible to visit all the places in heaven, even if it took a lifetime. The Lord than escorted me to show me some places. The Lord enjoyed taking me personally to show me the wonderful places of heaven.

RESTRICTED AREA IN HEAVEN

Jesus comforted me, "Bong-Nyo, despite your weakened condition, it will be difficult for you to witness. I know you have been emotionally dismayed." The Lord continued, "I have a special place to show you. This special place is permitted for only you. Observe carefully." I asked the Lord, "Where are You taking me?" He replied, "I will show you My Father's house. However, no one is allowed inside the house. You will only be able to see the exterior walls."

I remember the pastor teaching about God. The pastor once preached that God is light. God is the same yesterday, today, and forever. He will never change. God is with us, no matter where we are. He protects and looks after us.

I thought to myself, "How could God have a house?" The Lord pulled my hand and led me. We began to travel up toward the top of heaven. It seemed we flew endlessly upward. We reached a place where there were bright beams of light. We had reached the walls, which were made of pure gold. The whole wall, from bottom to top, was made out of pure gold.

Jesus told me that this area was restricted and that no one was allowed to approach it. The walls were very bright. I could not see clearly because of the light.

Jesus described that God is omnipresent, which means that He is everywhere at all times. Time does not affect God. He is involved in all aspects of His creation. He leads according to His will. The Lord continued to show me different places in heaven. He also crowned me with a golden crown. Thereafter we returned to The Lord's Church.

When I returned to church, I continued to pray. During my prayers, I saw a vision. I saw the throne of Father God. I was having a difficult time looking. The bright, rainbow-colored light was piercing my eyes. The light was very strong. I was not able to lift my head. As I was in prayer, I asked the Father, "Father God, why are You stretching toward me?" Then a voice of thunder that seemed to echo all around the world came from above. The gentle and authoritative voice said, "I just wanted to show you." When Father God stretched out, the world became brighter as it lit up with light.

Deaconess Shin Sung Kyung Joins the Prayer Rally

Deaconess Shin, Sung-Kyung: After our daytime prayer service, we all went to the pastor's house to eat. While I was eating, Sister Baek, Bong-Nyo told me that she had met Jesus and Yeh-Jee. She said that Yeh-Jee was in heaven with Jesus. I was shocked to hear that news. My daughter, Yeh-Jee, had a difficult life. She had battled cancer since kindergarten. She died at the age of nine at Han Yong University hospital. When she was most in pain, I had met Pastor Kim.

Before my daughter had cancer, I was in a cult. I was very devoted to the cult. However, I was able to get out of the cult once my daughter fell ill, as I had to spend more time taking care of her. My daughter was saved before she passed away. Pastor Kim was able to minister to her before her death. She had confessed with her mouth that Jesus was her Lord and Savior. She was in pain all the time. But when Pastor Kim arrived and prayed over her, her pain stopped. My daughter gently asked my husband and myself to hug her. After we had hugged her, she passed on and went to heaven. After she had died, she looked as though she were sleeping. The moment she died in peace, I knew there was a heaven. I then became a deaconess and devoted myself to the church. Unfortunately, I began working on Sundays after service. Every year, on the anniversary of Yeh-Jee's death, my husband and I would visit the island where her ashes are scattered. Today, we know that visiting the island is in vain.

Anyway, the prayer meeting consisted of nine people, and they prayed all night despite of the cold weather. They had told me that they met Jesus and had visited heaven and hell. To be honest, I really did not believe their claims or stories. However, the stories were not from one or two people; they all claimed it. Even the youngsters were spiritually awakened, and they were able to battle and cast out evil spirits. I would hear their revelations almost every week. I was embarrassed and ashamed to be associated with them and be called a deaconess. A sister who had only been attending this church for two months received the holy gift of tongues and prayed all night long. She had been spiritually awakened. As a newcomer, I saw her faith grow larger than mine. No one would have been able to figure out who was a new member and who was a deaconess.

I quit my job and decided to attend the all-night prayer sessions with a devoted heart. I was more shocked, and it was beyond my imagination or expectation. Even though I was a deaconess, I had not attended the nighttime prayer service. I also only gave half of my tenth in tithes. During my life, my prayers have been at best only ten minutes. After I had received the holy gift of tongues, I forced myself to pray for an hour.

When I arrived at the prayer meetings, I was shocked at what I witnessed. I was impressed with the night prayer service. They held prayer meetings every night. All of the adults and youngsters prayed until early morning without ceasing. Once they started, it usually lasted six hours. They did not even appear tired. The five year old, Meena, prayed for three hours straight. Meena even raised her arms and spoke in tongues. However, Meena sometimes fell asleep during her prayer in tongues.

I even brought my son to prayer nights. He was entering elementary school that year. My son was a troubled kid. He had already obtained a bad reputation among the neighbors. However, when he began attending, he pastor was very impressed to see my son at church with me. He was a renowned troublemaker.

OH, JUNG-MIN RECEIVES THE GIFT OF TONGUES

I had only attended Sunday services and was not aware of how different pastor's preaching was in the evenings. It was a shock to see the difference and the revelations revealed. The night preaching was not as calm as Sunday's preaching. With the Holy Spirit's manifestations, the preaching continued from 7:00 p.m. to 11:00 p.m. without a break.

The first thing I noticed was my son's behavior. My son, Jung-Min, usually cannot stay quiet or calm during Sunday service. It usually made me nervous and uncomfortable. However, with that night's service, he was glued to the pastor's sermon. It looked as though he had surrendered himself. He kept saying, "Amen, amen."

After the sermon, we began prayer service at 11:00 p.m. The pastor had designated a special place for my son. My son, Jung-Min, did not know how to pray. Therefore, the pastor began to explain to him about praying. The pastor provided a floor cushion and told him to sit on his knees, to raise his arms high, and pray without ceasing. Although my son was stubborn and ignorant, the pastor explained that he should pray with a desire in his heart and ask for the Holy Spirit's gift of tongues. The pastor explained that if he received the gift of tongues, he would be able to pray longer and receive power. The pastor directed him to ask and desire first for the gift of tongues.

Everyone was fervently praying in tongues. The pastor placed my son next to himself and told him to pray on the altar. The pastor laid hands on him and began to pray. As the pastor powerfully prayed over him, my son raised his arms high and began to cry. He then began to pray in tongues. My son was covered with tears and sweat.

I thought to myself, "He is only seven years old. How is it possible that he can repent and pray so earnestly?" I prayed to the Lord with a thankful heart. I decided to devote the rest of my time to the prayer meetings with all my heart. I then finished my prayer.

WILL CONTINUE IN BOOK NUMBER TWO...

TO CONTACT THE AUTHOR

As a pastor, I have read many books about spiritual warfare. I use these to preach, to teach, and to apply to my daily life and on mission trips in different countries.

When I first heard about the book *Baptize by Blazing Fire*, I thought it would be just another one of "those" books with a different title. However, after reading the book I realized my old concept of spiritual warfare was totally wrong and that I had a blindfold over my spiritual eyes. I have read all five books of Pastor Kim's Baptize by Blazing Fire Series.

There are many spiritual warfare books sold in Christian bookstores around the world. Most of the authors rely on their own experiences while applying biblical theory. (It is appropriate to use biblical principles to fight against demonic spirits and the dark forces of evil.) However, *Baptize by Blazing Fire* is different. The Lord Jesus appeared to this small church personally and opened the spiritual eyes of each member of the church. When their spiritual eyes were opened, they could see Jesus and demons. The Lord taught them how to fight against and resist the devil and his evil spirits while being able to actually see them. It was fascinating to know how easy it is to fight against the devil once your spiritual eyes are opened. There are so many demonic spirits around to cause sickness, evil thinking, family brokenness, church divisions, and so much more.

My reading prompted me to visit The Lord's Church in Korea, which I was able to do recently. I received a warm welcome from Pastor Kim, Yong-Doo and his congregation. My doubts about things written in the book evaporated like steam as I talked with Pastor Kim, others who were visiting, and the young people there. What amazed me is that the church is packed with prayer warriors starting at 9:30 p.m.

until 5:00 a.m. daily, 365 days a year. They are engaged in intercessory prayer. Every night there is powerful worship, spiritual dance, sermons, the impartation of anointing fire, and much prayer.

I have witnessed that Pastor Kim is taken to hell by the Lord at early dawn every day. The Lord Jesus wants him to experience the suffering and torment of hell because the Lord wants him to tell the world that hell is real. He was also taken to heaven many times. The Lord grieves that today's churches do not believe in hell or, at best, take it lightly.

This amazing book is a must-read for all Christians. *Baptize by Blazing Fire* will encourage you to overcome the spiritual battle as well as give you a wonderful foretaste of heaven.

My church intends to translate Pastor Kim's series of books into English. This will benefit many Christians in the world and give them the opportunity to translate them into their own languages.

My special thanks to Yoojin and Jena for their obedience and all the time they sacrificed to work on the translation of the book. (Recently, God has given them the gift of spiritual dance during their prayer time.)

> Be sober, be vigilant; because your adversary the devil, as a roaring lion, walketh about, seeking whom he may devour.
> —1 Peter 5:8

A bondservant of Jesus Christ,

—Pastor Michael Park
AMI Mission Church
(714) 537–3397
amisbuso@sbcglobal.net